WRITERS AND THEIR WORK

ISOBEL ARMSTRONG
*General Editor*

BRYAN LOUGHREY
*Advisory Editor*



# HENRY JAMES

HENRY JAMES

*from a portrait by* J. S. SARGENT *of 1913*
*National Portrait Gallery, London*

# HENRY JAMES

## *The Later Writing*

**Barbara Hardy**

NORTHCOTE

BRITISH COUNCIL

ATLANTIC
PUBLISHERS & DISTRIBUTORS (P) LTD

To Janet El-Rayess

This edition is published by

**ATLANTIC**

PUBLISHERS & DISTRIBUTORS (P) LTD

7/22, Ansari Road, Darya Ganj, New Delhi-110 002
Tel: 40775252, 23273880, 23275880, 23280451; Fax: +91-11-23285873
E-mail: orders@atlanticbooks.com; Web: www.atlanticbooks.com

By arrangement with
**Northcote House Publishers Ltd**
Horndon House, Horndon, Tavistock, Devon, PL19 9NQ,
United Kingdom. (T)+44(0)1822 810066; (F)+44(0)1822 810034
(E) northcote.house@virgin.net and (W) www.northcotehouse.co.uk
The *Writers and their Work* series is published in association with the British Council.


**First Indian Reprint 2010**
First published in 1996 by Northcote House Publishers Ltd

ISBN 978-81-269-1289-6



**British Library Cataloguing-in-Publication Data**
A catalogue record for this book is available from the British Library

Typeset by PDQ Typesetting, Newcastle-under-Lyme
Printed in India at Nice Printing Press, A-33/3A, Site-IV,
Industrial Area, Sahibabad, Ghaziabad, U.P.

# Contents

# Biographical Outline

1843 Henry James born at Washington Place, New York. His father, Henry James, Senior, inherited a share of his father's fortune of $3,000,000; studied in Princeton Theological Seminary; underwent life-changing experience of 'vastation' (as did his son, William, b. 1842); studied Swedenborg; wrote on theology and philosophy; travelled in Europe, giving his sons a 'sensuous', and cosmopolitan education, after trying schools in New York; married Mary Robertson Walsh, of Irish and Scottish descent, a Calvinist, and a strong, though conventional, wife and mother.

1845 Garth Wilkinson James born.

1846 Robertson James born.

1848 Alice James born. James wrote that girls had no chance in their family, and his sister's 'tragic health', chronicled, like her creativity, in her journal, shows how right he was.

1855–8 and 1859 Henry and brothers taught by tutors and governesses in London and Paris, and attend schools in France, Switzerland, and Germany.

1860 Henry attends Newport studio of William Morris Hunt but soon gives up.

1861 Fighting a fire at Newport, suffers a back injury, described by him as an 'obscure hurt', and perhaps a reason for not joining the Union Army in the Civil War.

1862–3 Attends Harvard Law School.

1864 In February publishes first story, 'A Tragedy of Error', unsigned, in the *Continental Monthly*, and first novel, *Watch and Ward* (1870), in the *Atlantic*. In the autumn his first known review, unsigned, appears in the *North American Review*, followed by reviews in it and the *Nation*.

| | |
|---|---|
| 1869–75 | Spends much of this period travelling in Europe. |
| 1870 | His cousin Mary ('Minny') Temple dies of tuberculosis at the age of 24. |
| 1875 | Lives in Paris for a year, making the acquaintance of Flaubert, Maupassant, Zola, and Turgenev. |
| 1876 | Takes lodgings in 3 Bolton Street, Piccadilly, and begins intense social life, becoming 'a Londoner', at home in England. |
| 1878 | Elected to Reform Club. |
| 1882 | His mother dies in January, and his father in December. James inherits a share of the estate. |
| 1894 | The novelist Constance Fenimore Woolson, a close friend, dies, perhaps committing suicide. |
| 1897 | Begins to dictate his work, continuing to do so for the rest of his life. |
| 1898 | Buys lease of Lamb House in Rye, Sussex. |
| 1899 | Meets Hendrik Andersen, a Boston sculptor, and forms a close friendship. Buys freehold of Lamb House. |
| 1903 | Charmed by Jocelyn Persse, and begins another warm friendship. Calls on Edith Wharton, beginning their friendship. |
| 1904 | Visits America after gap of about twenty years. |
| 1907–9 | New York Edition of the Novels and Tales. |
| 1909 | Meets Hugh Walpole. |
| 1910 | After a depressive illness and sudden recovery, goes to America with William and his family. William dies and Henry stays for nearly a year, visiting New York and other places, returning to England in 1911. |
| 1913 | Gives up room in Reform Club, and rents 21, Carlyle Mansions, Cheyne Walk, London, spending his remaining summers in Rye. |
| 1914 | Outbreak of First World War; James visits war-wounded in hospital. Awarded O.M. |
| 1915 | Is hurt by H. G. Wells's novel *Boon*, which makes a savage attack on his work, and writes dignified letters of protest and argument, on which Wells comments inadequately. |
| 1915 | Becomes naturalized British citizen. |
| 1916 | Dies, in February. Cremated at Golders Green, his ashes being buried in family plot in Cambridge. |

# References and Abbreviations

In view of the proliferation of James editions, references to quotations from his novels are by book and chapter. The three major novels discussed in this work – *The Ambassadors, The Wings of the Dove*, and *The Golden Bowl* – and the two unfinished novels – *The Sense of the Past* – and *The Ivory Tower* – are all in the New York Edition of 1907–18, from which all quotations are taken. The Penguin editions of the first three reproduce the text of the New York Edition.

Full details of editions of these and the other novels are given in the Select Bibliography.

Quotations from James's stories are all from *The Complete Tales of Henry James*, ed. Leon Edel (London: Rupert Hart-Davis, 1962–4)

Apart from the lecture 'The Lesson of Balzac' (which can be found in *The Question of Speech, The Lesson of Balzac: Two Lectures* (Boston and New York: Houghton, Mifflin, 1905), quotations from James's critical writings are all taken from *Henry James: The Critical Muse: Selected Literary Criticism*, ed. Roger Gard (Harmondsworth: Penguin, 1987).

The following abbreviations are used in the text:

*AS* *The American Scene*, intro. W. H. Auden (New York: Scribner's, 1946)
*CM* *Henry James: The Critical Muse: Selected Literary Criticism*, ed. Roger Gard (Harmondsworth: Penguin, 1987)
*Life* *Leon Edel, The Life of Henry James*, 2 vols. (Harmondsworth: Penguin, 1977)
*NSB* *Notes of a Son and Brother* (London: Macmillan, 1914)
*SBO* *A Small Boy and Others* (London: Macmillan, 1913)

# Introduction

In this brief account of Henry James's twentieth-century life and writing, I have combined a scan of his last fifteen years' work in every major literary genre except poetry, with a close reading of 'The Jolly Corner', *The Ambassadors, The Wings of the Dove, The Golden Bowl,* and *The Sacred Fount*. I have concentrated on two recurring subjects, history and imagination.

One of the most inward-looking of novelists, James is concerned with the determination and construction of identity. Like Madame Merle in *The Portrait of a Lady,* though disinterestedly, he asks, 'What shall we call our "self"? where does it begin? where does it end?' (ch. 19). His subject is the self and what Madame Merle calls 'the whole envelope of circumstances' and the enquiry into circumstances is increasingly occupied with the politics of women's and men's restriction and liberation. The last decade and a half, from 1900 to his death in 1916, is also the period when he shows most complexly his implicit and explicit interest in creativity and imagination. The themes are associated: James shows imagination as a means of seeing the socially constructed and restricted self, in a pragmatic and particular way. Some characters, like Strether and Merton Densher, dissociate themselves, choosing neutrality; others, like Maggie Verver, achieve a measure of liberation. Such visions are not mimetic. His characters, like their author, conduct an enquiry into experience, tentatively and provisionally, with a clear reflexive sense of narrative imagination's fiction and fantasy. Their self-awareness refracts their author's. While not suggesting that his subject is restricted, I have concentrated on these linked themes, one external, one internal, in a close reading of reflexive language and structure in examples of his later art.

I have not taken the works in chronological order, but grouped them according to genre, after beginning with 'The Jolly Corner', a story written in 1908, later than the three major novels. I consider it a model text which lucidly expresses the themes of history and imagination, and teaches us how to read James by highlighting his use of reflexive narrative and imagery. I concentrate on this story and four of the novels, but also say something about other late stories, two unfinished novels, plays, biography, travel-writing, and autobiographies. Finally, I have discussed his literary criticism, believing that he virtually created modern structural analysis of fiction and exercised a strong influence on judgements of Victorian and modern novels. A complete discussion of later James would take in his twentieth-century revisions of nineteenth-century texts, but I have excluded the subject, the less reluctantly because it is examined in Philip Horne's recent *Henry James and Revision*, a subtle book which contributes to James scholarship in more ways than its title suggests. My subject is the later writing, but I have borne in mind the artist's development and frequently referred to earlier work.

I have looked back to my first readings of James in *The Appropriate Form* (1964), in which I admired his achievements but argued against the constricting structural concepts of the New Criticism, Jamesian in affinity and to some extent in origin. There is no longer any need to criticize the terms in which James discussed his work, generalized about his genre, and evaluated uncongenial forms and conventions of Victorian fiction, but it is still appropriate to describe his books in some of the ways he taught us. And having recognized limitation in his theories, we can sort out valuable aspects. His ideals of tight unity and total relevance fit his own work, though they are no longer critically dominant, but other structural concepts explicit or implicit in his novels, prefaces, and essays anticipate later insights and ideas, especially concerns with dramatization of narrative voice, with reader-activity, and with reflexivity. My purpose is not to flatter James by reading him in the light of modern theoretical concerns but to recognize the interest of his concepts, in theory and in practice.

James stopped writing eighty-five years ago but is in some ways our contemporary, though it seems patronizing to say so. Not only in views on structure, but in attitudes to gender and social class, he is more congenial to late-twentieth-century critics of social injustice, capitalist values, and sexism than is often suggested.

The themes of history and imagination are integral to his modernity, one anticipating rejections of essentialism, the other articulating self-reference. Not as easy to press into the imaginary mould of the 'classic realist' author as George Eliot, his immediate predecessor in reflexive art, James reveals processes of fictionality with a brilliantly self-conscious turn. His self-consciousness never becomes abstraction. An intellectual force, and a novelist who offers problems and obscurities, he is a witty and sensuous writer, delighting his readers as he makes them work. He is a happily painstaking artist, original to the point of strangeness.

# 1

# Writing and Life, 1900–1916

Henry James was a Victorian, an Edwardian, and a modernist. His career is a progress and a continuity, not chopped up into tidy literary-historical periods, but its dense complexity makes chronological separation valuable, especially in a short study. Though all his writing is original and innovative, the last period is exceptionally rich and full.

James died on 28 February 1916, and in the fifteen years of his twentieth-century life became one of the inaugurators of a new epoch. His experiments in fictional voice and form break away from the structures of Victorian fiction to group themselves contemporaneously and proleptically with new form-makers and form-breakers like Conrad – whom James admired with reservations – and Lawrence, whom James did not admire. His new way with point of view, conclusion, symbolism, and pronounced formal features, which became more daring in the late work, anticipates Joyce, Dorothy Richardson, Woolf, Mann, and Beckett.

The mass and range of his later work are as impressive as their novelty: into the last decade and a half he crammed three of the most remarkable novels in European and American literature, two smaller novels, a number of good stories, his long three-part autobiography, reassessments of his European ancestors and contemporaries, Balzac, Flaubert, Turgenev and Zola, some of the most influential and analytic criticism of fiction ever written, a biography, travel-writing, essays, reviews, lectures, and two fascinatingly unfinished novels. He supervised the big New York Edition of his *Novels and Tales* published between 1907 and 1909, for which he made extensive revisions, but gained few rewards in sales or appreciation. He looked back on his Victorian identity and, in Yeats's phrase, remade himself, startlingly and appropriately, since the remaking of self is his recurring subject. He was aware that to remake is to unmake, jokingly using the franglais verb *se blottir*, though clarifying rather than expunging. He is piercingly alive to transformation, feeling its processes in the brain and thinking them in the nerves. He loves to transform characters – Brydon, Strether, Kate, Merton Densher, Amerigo, Maggie. He loves transformation scenes – in gardens, parks, drawing-rooms, theatres, and galleries. He himself transforms language and perception. Like Kafka and Beckett, he breaks routines of seeing and speaking, urging language and form into new categories. He takes us like his people into new regions. In one of the best 'homage' poems ever written, 'At the Grave of Henry James', W. H. Auden, who imitated the late prose in Caliban's virtuoso address in *The Sea and the Mirror*, celebrated James as 'master of nuance and scruple': it is the scrupulously nuanced self-generative voices and visions of his imaginative characters that make him a language-changer and a life-changer.

Like Beckett, for similar reasons, he is not for all tastes. His analytic method makes him difficult reading. Beckett jokingly addresses the 'gentle skimmer' and James is also scornful about readers who skip rather than read words. A colleague of mine, the philosopher Richard Peters, compared reading James to reading Kant and Wittgenstein. We cannot read him without changing the pace and mode of our thinking. So some readers give up, impatient or exhausted. He is like Beckett in his strenuous style – James loves the word 'strenuous', speaking of the novelist 'at his strenuous hour' – and we must make strenuous efforts to read him. James's originality – rather, his oddity – also makes him difficult, like Beckett, Hopkins, Purcell, Messiaen, Giacometti, and all artists whose work is marked with mannerism, extravagance, or strangeness. Since the Russian formalist Shklovsky publicized his concept of *ostranenie*, the idea of defamiliarization or 'making strange' has become a critical commonplace. It is a useful one, especially if we take it back to Coleridge's *Biographica Literaria*, where what looks like a brilliant statement of the obvious is fined down into distinctions between individual artists. James's defamiliarizations are more Coleridgean than Wordsworthian, forms of fantasy often dominating, but he is also strange in being highly idiosyncratic. His strangeness is probably as much temperament as art. He is one of those artists who meditates on experience so strongly and strangely, and who feels and thinks so strongly and strangely about his art, that he moves form and language to extremes. To experience extremity and be compelled by strangeness can be unnerving, though also – to use James's word for what he hoped to share with us – 'fun'.

James offers readers his strangeness at a price. Like Lewis Carroll's Humpty-Dumpty, he rewards hard work. If there are readers who cannot stand him, there are those for whom he is the great novelist to be preferred above Dickens, George Eliot, Stendhal, Tolstoy, and Joyce – whoever your top five may be. If you are one of the readers for whom he seems intolerably mannered, it is worth trying him again from time to time: he may seem to improve or change as we improve or change.

To read James the story-teller at his strangest, in his last period, is to contemplate the perfection of a genre and a style. Perfection is a word which should be no sooner uttered than revised. Of course there are flaws. James is sufficiently radical as a critic of society to make us wish he were more radical. Some of his attitudes, especially to race and class (not, I think to gender) are or seem intolerant and superior. Of course he is constrained by his time, but like Jane Austen, with whom he has a lot in common, he is so aware of historical conditioning that we expect him to rise above the cultural norms. But his failures exist side by side with his successes and efforts. Given special emphasis by being refracted through his characters, the efforts are persistent and subtle.

Historical determinism is a central subject of the Victorian novelists, but the two most famous succumbed to optimism. Dickens's capitalist Dombey and his ideal gentleman Wrayburn overcome the constrictions of their culture to achieve ideal selflessness and love; and though Eliot's Dorothea Ladislaw is deliberately undermined as an achiever, and Daniel Deronda allowed only a 'vague' if 'grand' conclusion, an unmistakable note of moral admiration sounds at the end of their fictional careers. James may have such ancestors and contemporaries in mind when he writes in 'The Art of Fiction' (1884) (*CM*, no. 26): 'As for the aberrations of a shallow optimism, the ground (of English fiction especially) is strewn with their brittle particles as with broken glass.'

James is more conscious of historical restraint than Dickens and

Eliot, closer to Thackeray and Hardy in his social discontents. *The Portrait of a Lady* (1881), though morally affirmative, is a dark novel. Its heroine renounces desire and chooses altruism, but the conclusion is dispirited and distressed in a way *Middlemarch* is not. Dorothea's is a sunrise vision, Isabel feels enclosed by the 'grey curtain of her indifference' (ch. 53). There is no jumping for joy at the end of most James novels, as there can be even in the death-scenes of Dickens and Eliot. Exceptional in its happy ending, *The Golden Bowl* is problematic precisely because of its rewards and punishments. From his second novel, *Roderick Hudson* – which he called his first, since *Watch and Ward* is relatively slight – the long fictions of the early and middle years are mostly studies in instructive failure, tragically and comically frustrating or corrupting character by circumstance.

I do not think James's avoidance of progressivist faiths has a single source in historical insight. He was not a Christian, though he hankered after self-sacrifice, but his intelligent sense of history observed and invented historical causalities for renunciations. Hardy said some natures become vocal in the face of tragedy, and James clearly needs to imagine renunciations, especially of love. (If he had a homosexual novel in a secret drawer, like Forster, it might have been, like *Maurice*, indulgent rather than strenuously imaginative.) His consistent urge to imagine sexual losses, betrayals, and sacrifices provokes biographical questions, but no certain answers. We can suggest that sexual problems shape his art, that he shed his sicknesses – if he had sicknesses – in his novels. Leon Edel suggests that, after meeting Hendrik Andersen, Jocelyn Persse, and Hugh Walpole, in later life, James found himself able to admit, if not consummate, a suppressed homosexuality, so comes in the late novels to renounce renunciation. I agree that there is a new exhilaration, even triumph, in the last three novels, but I think Edel's highly speculative reading of life and art ignores the renunciations in *The Ambassadors*, and *The Wings of the Dove*, as well as James's defence in 'The Lesson of the Master', however ambiguous, of an ideal celibate solitude for art.

Of course our ignorance of the reticent novelist's private life may lead us to invent a story of celibacy and non-attachment. We tend to identify James with Strether's sense of missing the train, but the speech urging life on Little Bilham is based on the words of W. D. Howells, not James, who told Hugh Walpole to 'wallow, or splash, or plunge, or dizzily and sublimely soar (into the jinks element)':

> It's good healthy exercise, when it comes but in bouts and brief convulsions, and it's always a kind of thing that it's good, and considerably final to *have* done. We must know, as much as possible, in our beautiful art, yours and mine, what we are talking about – and the only way to know is to have lived and loved and cursed and floundered and enjoyed and suffered. (Quoted in *Life*, ii. 697)

This robust and matter-of-fact defence of indulgence should be written out a hundred times by those believing James may have suffered 'from an insufficiency of physical experience', as Tony Tanner suggests in his *Henry James III*, (p. 9). Leon Edel quotes this passage two pages after 'With James there is always a touch of "too late, too late"', which introduces another of James's bracing retrospects: '"I think I don't regret a single 'excess' of my responsive youth, I only regret in my chilled age, certain occasions and possibilities I didn't embrace"' (*Life*, ii. 694). Neither remark is the defence or regret of a celibate recluse. Even if the anecdote about him turning down Hugh Walpole with 'I can't' is true, it does not mean he never could or never did. It may seem odd to have high jinks celebrated because they contribute to the art of fiction, but that is another story. There are passages in *The Wings of the Dove* and *The Golden Bowl* which I find it hard to imagine emanating from R. D. Laing's hyper-conscious 'unembodied self' which Tanner thinks 'might be relevant'. James's words to Grace Norton in 1884 about feeling advanced in happiness and power since deciding not to marry, and his admission to Edmund Gosse in 1903 that he is gleeful at not having *bambini*, but aware of missing something, sound in no way neurotic.

Whatever the cause, the pressure on his fictions and his characters to imagine sexual and emotional deprivations brings with it a sense of history. I think this gets more explicit in the later years, when James's political consciousness seems to strengthen with the habitual retrospects of age, the return journey to America in 1904, and the long experience of art's enquiry. Many characters in the earlier fiction – Rowland Mallett, Christopher Newman, Isobel Archer, Fleda Vetch – are denied final gratifications, but their descendants – Strether, Milly Theale – are even more illustratively unfulfilled. There are the transitional cases of *Daisy*

*Miller*, with its incompatibly determined narrator and heroine, and *The Awkward Age*'s Nanda Brookenham, whose conservation by old Mr Longdon turns novel into parable. One is a short fiction, the other strains the sense of probability. The later works perfectly blend realism with illustration. Radical unachievers are exemplary and dominant in the last novels and tales, and the apparent exceptions, Spencer Brydon of 'The Jolly Corner', and Maggie Verver, are not totally joyous affirmations, and one is revealed by fantasy, as half a divided ego, the other wins a Pyrrhic victory.

In his novels, James only once deals in the first person, unmediatedly, with the sexual or the social life, because his primary theme is imagination. When the first-person narrators of *The Turn of the Screw* and *The Aspern Papers* tell their stories, it is with an imaginative memory of the past, not necessarily unreliable, but placed and characterized, not authoritative. These tellers belong to the middle years. In the later period James presents characters concerned to imagine, as well as put or not put desire into action. He shows events through a filter or lens of individual memory, desire, illusion, or re-vision: to quote the wonderfully modern figure he used for Conrad's narrator, Marlow, in 'The New Novel' (*CM*, no. 76), he produces a 'prolonged hovering flight of the subjective over the outstretched ground of the case exposed', the 'shadow cast by the flight' (James had seen Blériot in the air). This is not an evasion: every artist presents life through a filter or lens of memory, desire, illusion, or re-vision. What James does is to acknowledge, place, motivate, individualize, and historicize the subjective presentation. This is why he insists in the Prefaces about a doubled pleasure for writer and reader, in the story narrated and the act of narration. And it is why he is so at ease in his art's integrity. It is a reflexive art which never strains to be artistically self-conscious because it imagines every character and every psychic event as imaginative. It is never reflexivity for its own sake, as a fashion, or a jolt of the reader into activity, as Roland Barthes sees it. James always has something worth reflecting and reflecting on in artistic self-consciousness.

The subject of the artistic or aesthetic life inhabits too small a region to contain James's drama of the imaginative life, though he frequently treats literature, painting, and sculpture in the short story, which he knew excluded development of character. There are only two novels concerned with the artist's life, *Roderick*

*Hudson*, whose central character, Rowland Mallett, is not an artist, and *The Tragic Muse*. The most common Jamesian figure is not an artist but a man or woman painfully aware of historical restraint, trying to imagine freedom. The historical awareness, I believe, becomes more pronounced in the later work, from 1900 until his death in 1916.

The last fifteen years of James's life were the first years of a new century, and he moved into it with fresh zest and self-generating creativity, in old and new genres of travel, biography, and autobiography, but above all in fiction and literary criticism. It was in those years that James played his star part in making the modern novel and modern analytic criticism. They were years when he put down roots, became a hospitable host and head of household, got to know and love his brother William's growing children, and made many new friends. He never became a popular or high-earning novelist, but found an increasing circle of genuinely appreciative readers, including new writers. James's last years were also marked by those common pains named by the ageing lively Yeats in 'The Tower', 'wreck of body', 'decay of blood', and 'death of friends'. He suffered from increasing ill health – gout, shingles, bad teeth, stomach trouble, nervous tension, depression, a bad breakdown, and constant anxieties about the body's failure. He looked ahead, as everyone who lives long enough must look, down the 'black avenue'.

One of the most important things that happened in his late years was the return journey to America in 1904. Visiting the changed New York of his boyhood, the Boston he knew so well, and many states for the first time, was a harsh experience which became art. His records of the American scenes are bruised and shocked but always controlled by humour and irony. James remained the tireless traveller: *The American Scene* tells a story of ten months' strenuous observing, walking, interviewing, visiting, lecturing, travelling by train, and motoring. He disliked the pollution and stench of the motor car but appreciated access to new places and pleasures. His new friends included Edith Wharton – whose luxurious cars he enjoyed and whose organizing generosity he appreciated or tolerated – Stephen Crane, Conrad, Wells, and the attractive young men, Hugh Walpole and Jocelyn Persse, with whom he enjoyed his own kind of effusive friendship. He loved his extended family, having fun with his nephews and nieces, the perfect avuncular host. He got on well with his devoted servants, and, though his paternalism may offend modern tastes, it seems to spring from affection and sweetness rather than superiority. 'Brooksmith', a story about a manservant who loses his occupation, is to my mind a less patronizing and pessimistically manipulative treatment of a servant's servitude than *The Remains of the Day*. During the war his letters to his manservant and his hospital visits to soldiers show the active and unaffected kindness so often mentioned by his friends.

He still enjoyed holidays in Paris and Italy, but the last years were divided between London and Rye, where in 1898 he bought Lamb House, living there on and off till his death. Rye gave him a familial and citizenly sense of belonging to a household and a community, though at times he felt immobilized and incarcerated there, and always needed London. After 1900 he had a room in the Reform Club, and in 1913 he bought a flat, 21, Carlyle Mansions, Cheyne Walk, where his seventieth birthday that year was celebrated with letters, cables, telegrams, flowers, a portrait by John Singer Sargent, a bust by a young sculptor, Derwent Wood, and a golden bowl. A little earlier, the generous, admiring, and tactless Edith Wharton tried to organize a presentation purse, and James cabled his nephew, Billy James, 'Please express to individuals approached my horror money absolutely returned' (*Life*, ii. 75).

The First World War caused him deep distress, and led to his naturalization as a British citizen in 1915. He was signalling sympathy for his adopted country, and also avoiding the wartime inconveniences of immigrant status. James's worst social despondency is summed up in an article he wrote for the *New York Times* in February 1915, in which he laments language-loss: '. . . we are now confronted with a depreciation of all our terms . . . with a loss of expression through increase of limpness, that may well make us wonder what ghosts will be left to walk' (*Life*, ii. 788).

But he had been despairing before, after his failures in the theatre during the 1890s, in 1904 when he contemplated the future of his country, and often when observing the success of other writers. It is interesting to compare his sense of isolation and critical neglect with that of Hardy, who gave up novel-writing after

1899, whereas James, who contemplated giving it up, went on to write – rather dictate, to secretaries who typed as he spoke, encouraging his relaxed fluid self-qualifying conversational style – his best novels and the remarkable autobiographies in which he reimagined distress. He suffered from neglectful critics and readers more than Hardy: Hardy was attacked by shocked hypocrites, but James was rejected, ridiculed and patronized, well into this half-century. Hardy offended by candour, James by mannered and intricate obscurity. Though the poor sales of the New York Edition were bitterly disappointing, his last years were full and strenuous. Apart from his fiction and reviews, there was a voluminous and entertaining correspondence, a preface to Rupert Brooke's posthumously published *Letters from America*, and lectures, including the highly praised 'On the Novel in *The Ring and the Book*' (*CM*, no. 73). No wonder he was incredulous at Shakespeare's early retirement. James was dictating on his death-bed.

He suffered two strokes, and his elaborate ramblings, elegantly phrased but pathologically hallucinated or nonsensical, are his only wild words. He went on making writing movements in his last coma, before he died on 28 February 1916.

# 2

# 'The Jolly Corner': Theme and Model

'The Jolly Corner' teaches us how to read James. I take it out of chronological order as a matrix of themes and a structural model. It epitomises late James. Published in 1908, it is a subtly reflexive story, a paradigm in more ways than one.

It is a ghost story in which fantasy reveals the terrifying and pitiable ghosts we all see, as present is haunted by past, actuality by possibility, has-been by might-have-been. There are two famous examples of a romantic version of this fantasy, Charles Lamb's brilliantly pathetic 'Dream Children', in which the childless bachelor imagines beloved issue, and James Barrie's *Dear Brutus*, in which an unborn child sighs that she does not want to be a might-have-been. Lamb's pathos is successful, his ghosts particularized to articulate the gain and loss of imagined intimacy. Even in Barrie's soft romance there is the sheer interest of the idea, the tugging strength of myth beneath sentimentality.

James's ghost is highly individualized, like Lamb's dream children, and his specificity engages sympathy for haunter as well as haunted. Unlike Lamb's rapt little listeners, Spencer Brydon's might-have-been or other self is an unwanted, threatening, and dreaded revenant, though he becomes sympathetic in the end, in a way. We feel for ghost as well as ghost-seer, because we feel for a whole person, a person whole enough to imagine his own alternative history. Like most of James's protagonists, Brydon has to be remade, and for him, as for Strether in *The Ambassadors*, remaking involves imagining what he might have been in other circumstances, seeing, if not accepting, his potential greed, corruption, violence, and suffering. But it is not a simple fable of moral division, like *Dr Jekyll and Mr Hyde* or *The Picture of Dorian*

*Gray*. Brydon's ghost has to be understood as vulnerable as well as powerful, human as well as monstrous, familiar as well as strange.

This story is a fable of the split psyche, historical determinacy, and creativity. Its genre, narration, and image-making are reflexive. It is necessary to the story's point that the ghost is raised – and is seen to be raised – by the ghost-seer. The fantasy is facilitated at the beginning by the hero's act of imagination, an act which is psychological and political: the ghost of a man who has never lived is raised to demonstrate the social construction of character. The refined Europeanized exile confronts the crude American businessman, perceived as aggressive and aggressed, a gangster and a scarred victim of violence. The story works through two characters, the woman, for whom this perception is easy, and the man, for whom it is hard. It is through Brydon's imagination that the ghost walks, but it is through Alice Staverton's capacity for loving and dreaming that his cruelty and power are accepted as human. The acceptance is the opposite of romantic.

I think it is James's best love-story, and, like his first strange novel, *Watch and Ward*, it has a rare happy ending. Perhaps such a conclusion could be best worked out for him in allegory, though the allegory is fleshed out, like the ghost story. The ghost is imagined by the woman who is outside, and the man who is his double or *alter ego*. He is loved by the woman, as well as eventually acknowledged by the man, as a part or a potentiality of the self, and it is one of James's profound insights to see love as an acceptance which grasps the actual and sees the potential. What makes it a good love-story is the capacity to make love strange, to tell new truths about love.

Disfigured by a violence which is symbolic and realistic, the ghost, a 'black stranger', like Conrad's Mr Kurtz, is a darkness in the crude New York culture. James's ghost-seer is a sensitive Europeanized American exile. Returning to find his roots, he finds a horror rooted inside himself. It is the killer or torturer inside us all, the shadow-self a humanist might deny. It is an alternative construction, a creature of another history. Its virility is attractive to the woman, and also to the imagination of Brydon, drawn to the brute sexuality of which Strether scents a tigerish whiff in Gloriani's Parisian garden. Because the ghost is an unacknowledged and unacted aspect of Brydon, Brydon is made responsible for his evocation. James – contemporary of Freud – imagines a self-analysis in which the buried self is released. Brydon's black stranger is the repressed and desired self which haunted the Victorians, in a haunting which is political as well as sexual. Gerard Hopkins imagines Tom Navvy and admits to Robert Bridges that, in a way, he sympathizes with Communism; Dickens invents the wild revolutionary glee of Hugh and Barnaby and the lusts of Quilp and Pecksniff. Arnold feels the bolt shoot back in the breast; there are Jekyll's Hyde and Dorian's portrait; and later on Adela Quested's sexual and racist hallucination in the Marabar cave.

The myth of the forbidden and buried self, with its mutually reinforcing psychic and political significance, finds expression as James's intelligence confronts a historical alternative and unacted passions. Hopkins and Dickens ambivalently imagine revolution; Forster, Wilde, and Arnold conceive mask and anti-self. Sexual and political subversions join. James intuits these junctions in a story, like Conrad's *The Secret Sharer*, which recognizes the social construction of our lives. Nowhere else did James so shockingly figure our insubstantiality, our lack of an essential self, as when he made Brydon see the scarred and half-blinded face of his alternative, repressed self, the shadow-side of civilized man, with its greed, violence, virility, and suffering. He knew exactly what he was doing. Amongst other things, he was writing a fable for over-liberated and unliberated men.

The story is about story-telling, about fantasy, about the capacity to see darkness in the daylight. James's reflexivity is instructive, never merely aesthetic. He may have started with a simple idea about the *alter ego* as a crude capitalist image, and his ghost gathered passion in the imagining, to become more bestial, sinister, and gross, but more habitable as a possible other. Perhaps the impulse to demonize the alternative self overreached itself and forced recognition: the traditionally destructive ghost which seems to urge suicide shows a way to love. Brydon is driven into a coma, and wakes with his head on Alice's breast.

The story is about the drive to create fantasy, and it is a good fantasy, thrilling us with terror and pity. It is told with great skill, and like all the best ghosts, its ghost emerges with uncanny stealth. It can be read as James's revision of *The Turn of the Screw*, because it knows, as the earlier story did not quite dare to know, that ghosts are inside us. (Because *The Turn of the Screw* made its ghosts external, many critics, including Edmund Wilson, adroitly, and Leon Edel, maladroitly, have rewritten them into the governess's 'neurotic' fantasy, in a projection which seems to me blatantly sexist.) James created this projection in Brydon, as he had in another male character, 'Owen Wingrave', another story of the divided self, and another exemplary tale in which an extreme of masculine violence destroys its tender and better half. 'The Jolly Corner' revises this story too.

Spencer Brydon utters the *fiat*, the words of creative will, 'Let there be' – in this case 'Let there be a ghost'. Like James himself, the character transforms metaphor into actuality, with a transitional phase when he formulates a hypothesis or entertains a belief. Of course both metaphor and actuality are fictional, but the levels of fictitiousness are differentiated as we see the character at his imaginative work. First he uses a metaphor, almost without thinking, next takes thought, then starts off a story within the story, a story of his own, to represent his author, inspect the theme of imagination, and develop power over the character he invokes. The process of creation is slow and gradual, right for the raising of spirits. Like Yeats the spiritualist, James imagined materialization as a hard and painful process for the spirit. Like Shakespeare the dramatist, he knew how slow motion makes the flesh creep.

The jolly corner is established as a New York site, then physical place figures inner space, 'he scarce knew what to make of this lively stir, in a compartment of his mind never yet penetrated, of a capacity for business . . .'. The dead metaphors of 'compartment' and 'penetrate' are joined by the innocently revived 'lively stir' but prepare less innocent and less lively stirring in a space not yet penetrated. Brydon contemplates his surprising new capacity for business: 'If he had stayed at home', jokes Alice, 'he would have anticipated the inventor of the skyscraper'. (James detested skyscrapers.) Her words start the muffled 'vibration' of a 'wonderment', which 'met him like some strange figure, some unexpected occupant, at a turn of one of the dim passages of an empty house'. (James's free indirect style shares the transformation with the characters' direct speech.) The suggestive personification of 'wonderment', metaphor of 'compartment', and simile of 'figure' and 'turn', are reinforced by the Irish woman's fear of coming to the house in the 'ayvil' hours. Her accent is standardized in Brydon's assimilation 'evil', another small step in the making of a ghost. *Solvitur ambulando*, or 'the wheels take fire of their own motion', Coleridge's image of generative form.

Now the uncanny casually re-enters in a slang phrase: Brydon does not have 'the ghost' of a reason for living in New York. His dead metaphor is detained by Alice for revival, 'Are you very sure the 'ghost' of one doesn't, much rather, serve – ?', to elicit: 'Oh ghosts – of course the place must swarm with them!' This self-generating series of hints and cues prepares for questions about 'what he personally might have been'. Question leads to answer. This is good ghost-lore: ghosts, like some fairies and devils, must be asked to appear. The slow summoning includes a turn from image to event, invocation to apparition. The making of story and the raising of the ghost proceed together, but the ghosts are still in Brydon's inset story. He has been transforming ghosts of language, dead tropes, to live fantasy.

After he goes into the house, in the evil hours, to receive many impressions, there are uncanny physical manifestations of a closed door and an open door, which shift the haunting from inside to outside the mind. There is lavish use of the retarding element – a term we see James savouring in an essay on *Wilhelm Meister* (*CM*, no. 3). Brydon decides not to open the closed door, then moves expectantly through two rooms into a third, in a graduated approach which occurs again in another story of a haunted house in another country, *A Sense of the Past*. He turns his back on the upstairs room, goes down, feels trapped, looks down from a high window to imagine self-destruction, and escapes downstairs to find his ghost inside, on the threshold. Climax and revelation are still delayed as the ghost hides behind his hands, with tell-tale missing fingers, then shows a ravaged face to his other self. There is a source for this face in *The Golden Bowl*, when Maggie figures the evil that has suddenly arrived in her home, 'evil seated . . . where she had only dreamed of good' in an image-narrative she gradually generates: 'it had met her like some bad-faced stranger surprised in one of the thick-carpeted corridors of a house of quiet' (bk. V. ch. 2). The bad-faced stranger has changed by the time he is surprised on the jolly corner.

Alice Staverton, on whose breast Brydon recovers from nightmare, trauma, and swoon, says she saw the other man first, in a dream, then, priestess-like, judges that Brydon has been haunted not by a might-have-been but by something 'never meant to be'. She pronounces her acceptance of the *alter ego*, 'how could I not have liked him?' Her act of integration is made by a lover's imagination, in spite of those diabolical and monstrous aspects of 'the black stranger'. In retrospect, the urge to destruction and the repugnance make good sense, projected fears of the psychic depths Brydon must plumb.

Matrix of themes and generative model, the story links with the earlier texts like *The Turn of the Screw*, and with 'The Beast in the Jungle', whose beast and haunting are manifested in metaphor, and whose desolate denial of love is overturned, as in another late love-story, 'The Bench of Desolation'. And there is a structural link with *The Golden Bowl*, a pattern of reversibility.

I once heard a radio story in which a woman had a recurring dream about a haunted house, to find as the dream came true that she had been the haunter. James had a nightmare set in the Louvre, which began with fear but ended with him telling a strange old man that he was afraid of the dreamer, not the other way round. (It is a fascinatingly different psychic experience from the 'vastation' suffered by his father and his brother.) James articulates this experience of reversed haunting in Brydon's consciousness. We are made to feel the story could be told and felt from the other self's point of view, and this makes psychic and political sense. Intimacy and alteriority are intensified; the relationship between the two halves or selves is more animated; and the sense of history articulated.

The maimed and ravaged millionaire, incapacitated for love – 'he has a million but he hasn't got you' – whose power is felt by the woman who also sees him, is a plausible rendering of an alternative self materializing from another dimension in sky-scraping new New York. The city being torn down and built up is the lucrative and destructive space in which he is imagined. It is his territory, the envelope of his self. Feeling is imputed to the apparition; fear, shame, and aggression are provoked by his alternative self as he provokes similar feelings in Brydon. The sense of reversibility has an intellectual effect, questioning the idea of essentialism and integrity of character, and a sensational effect, of strangeness. The reversible form is like Escher's ambiguous constructions, logical, neat, and weird, as it turns itself inside out, prompting us to imagine the story told from the viewpoint of the New York millionaire, contemplating his alternative history, hiding his face and hiding from the other face, hunted as well as hunter. It imagines otherness in an appropriate form.

James is said to have felt that 'The Jolly Corner' encroached on *The Sense of the Past*, and Ralph Pendrel's unfinished story is like Brydon's in this dynamic reversibility: Ralph is a time-traveller who feels the strangeness of the people he meets in the past, and also senses them feeling his uncanniness as a time-alien. *The Golden Bowl* creates a similar structure. The reversal of Amerigo's by Maggie's point of view habituates the mind to turnings, putting us in the right frame of mind to imagine her imagining her father working from his side, as she from hers, to manipulate discoveries and solutions without disclosure.

'The Jolly Corner' is James's richest tale, joining allegory and realism, historical and psychological analysis, figuring imagination mutedly and implicitly, unlike the artist-stories, 'The Figure in the Carpet', 'The Death of the Lion', and 'The Lesson of the Master'. The man and the woman in 'The Jolly Corner' are not artists, only human beings capable, in collaboration, of the strenuously analytic and synthetic act of imagining the self, the other, the psyche, and history. Through their figures James deals with sex, society, and art, and the self-consciousness of the artist's reflexive mode is subdued. The story is reflexive in a depth and a breadth which make it a congenial companion to the three great novels which precede it, and the unfinished ones James laid aside, *The Ivory Tower*, a story much concerned with money, and *A Sense of the Past*, another historical fantasy.

'The Jolly Corner' points to James's awareness of historical construction and relativism, his rejection of an absolutist sense of 'human nature', which becomes clearer in the late memoirs and fiction, despite his biographer's attempt to see him as a believer in psychological truth and human nature. Edel interprets an important exchange between Shaw and James as a debate between Shavian socialism and Jamesian essentialism. In 1909, when James's old theatrical ambitions were being encouraged, Shaw rejected 'The Saloon', the dramatized version of 'Owen Wingrave', on the grounds that it was depressingly and Darwinianly 'determinist', a no-hope image of military bondage and power. James's pacifist hero is defeated but ironically heroic, conditioned to brave the ancestral soldier-ghost, and in a preview of the Soviet literary debate between idealizing propaganda and realism, Shaw the socialist is on the side of propaganda, James the liberal on the side of historical analysis. Edel reads James's weak response to Shaw, – 'I do such things because I happen to be a man of imagination and taste... because the imagination... enjoys and insists on and incurably leads a life of its own...' – 'as a defence of 'the question of "human nature"' against Shaw's desire to make art serve revolution (*Life*, ii. 667–8). Lawrence says 'Never trust the artist, trust the tale', and I propose that James's story, far from asserting 'human nature' and Edel's vague 'psychological truths', embodies social pressures with a political intelligence that Shaw is too romantic, Edel too conventional, and James himself insufficiently politicized, to admit. James is at his most political when he is embodying, not discussing, political implications. 'The Jolly Corner' demonstrates his political intuition and intelligence with the clarity of fable.

# 3

# *The Sacred Fount* and *The Outcry*

*The Sacred Fount* was conceived as a short story, then published as a novel in 1901. Its action takes place over one weekend, on the train and in a country house, keeping the unity of time and place James uses with economy and force in his shorter fiction. It has the unusual feature of a first-person narrator, avoided in James's novels, as it was by George Eliot and Hardy. It is essential to this teasing story, because it lets James keep secrets in a way impossible for his usual narrator, who looks over his characters' shoulders and goes behind their backs. This narrator wants to look and go behind, and is not allowed to. It is a story which made Henry Adams say that Harry James should go to a 'cheery asylum' and irritated Edmund Wilson by its mystification. Several reviewers agreed that it was a departure from sanity, though they were also unsympathetic to James at his most accessible.

More riddling than the first-person narrative of *The Turn of the Screw*, it mingles comedy and poetry to create the nameless narrator's ambiguity. The reader never knows quite how to read him or his detective enterprise. Like James's best reflexive tale 'The Figure in the Carpet', it is a test and a tease, forcing us to admit hermeneutic defeat. We end not by knowing, as we expect in Victorian stories or modern whodunits, but by not knowing. It is an epistemological fable with a twist of unresolved mystification, a pre-parody of the three great late novels, with their symbolic stories of clandestine sex.

'The Figure in the Carpet' is a joke about curious critics. *The Sacred Fount* is a joke about curious readers who go to novels and gossip for salacious pleasure. The joke is licensed because it is also made at the expense of the complicit and curious author. James was a gossip, a kind man capable of spite and malice. Famous for not wanting to hear too much of those dinner-table anecdotes about a son fighting his mother over valuable furniture and *objets d'art*, and an Italianate American father with a little 'moulded daughter' and a 'massive' Tuscan villa, he exercised listening restraint only in the interests of stimulus and invention. His nameless narrator is like him in loving gossip, unlike him in not knowing where to stop.

Though the narrator speculates about couples in a hands-on manner, he has some dignity. The fount is sacred as well as profane, feeding the artist's curiosity, wonder, and speculation. As he says, 'imagination rides' him. James sees the funny side of story-seeking, to use his own phrase. But he sees its serious side too. The narrator is attacked for being far-fetched in speculation and vain of his talent for 'gouging' out secrets – an image James used of his own work – but praised for cleverness and pertinacity. If the narrator is a voyeur, it is of inward as well as outward life, and he has compassion and enough humour to see the joke against himself.

He is a theorist, his hypothesis formed as he is puzzled by changes in two fellow-travellers on their way by train to a weekend house party. The hospitality is the kind James describes so well in the novels that follow, and in such stories as 'Broken Wings', where two hard-up artists renew affinity among the lion-hunting rich. (The light satiric touch, ear for social chit-chat, and nose for *louche* atmosphere must have influenced the comic realism and fantasy of Evelyn Waugh and Saki.) As the unnamed narrator sees a dull man turn into a wit and a young husband age while his older wife puts on youth, he hatches the idea of a sacred fount, secretly nourishing and draining powers in close relationships, marriages, and dangerous *liaisons*. The wonderfully erotic and ironic symbol draws on the Muses' fountain as well as the fountain of Egeria, which supplied King Numa, and which James had visited.

The imaginative artist, whose negative capabilities are aptly anonymous, next conceives the possibility of spotting clandestine couples by making inferences from signs of reciprocity and exchange. The sacred fount also images the thirst of a narrator who drinks greedily from the fountain of inspiration. For him, no mere Peeping Tom but an artist, the imagination is sacred. His dignity is assured – perhaps defended is a safer word – by the excellence of his theory and perception, even as he starts and keeps up the weekend party game of 'spot the couple'. (It is a parlour game where the action is decorously staged downstairs.) Using the age-reversal of the Brissingham marriage as model, he theorizes and speculates with selected fellow-guests till at the end he is criticized and rejected by Mrs Brissingham, his chief collaborator. If readers have not already had doubts about her, they will start wondering when she angrily withdraws from the collaboration, no longer finding the game amusing, like someone overturning the *Monopoly* board in a rage.

Why does she want to stop playing? Is she on the point of giving her game away? Is she the missing woman who has fed Gilbert Long with her wit and intelligence, as well as the wife draining youth from her husband? Did she and Gilbert join the narrator on the train journey, and gossip with him about who is travelling with whom, as an effective cover? Is she the mouthpiece of James's interest in realism and point of view, when she tells the narrator the truth is not as he gouges it out, or is this hostility her fear? Has James written a detective story in which the guilty person hides her trail by parading her part as detective's aide? In that case, is she stupid or too clever? Does the collaborative gossip become hard to sustain? Does her withdrawal show she has overreached herself? Or has she come to believe that the narrator's hypothesis has been negated? And does he think he has found the solution as he deprecates his failure, ingenuously or disingenuously, at the end?

However we ask and answer, we have to go back or recall the story, like the lady reader Sterne sent back to reread the previous chapter. But because the narrator can only guess and infer, never know for certain, the speculative revisions can only oscillate, not conclude. We are only rewarded by seeing the joke, as the tables are turned on the powerful artist-figure and perhaps on the collaborator too. If we take the story seriously enough to pursue his speculation, we will not see the joke, but if we do see it, we may see the possibility that we are inventing it as a solution to a problem. Reader-response theory's insistence on the proliferation of response is a help; indeed, James often seems to anticipate the concept. Students sometimes invoke the Uncertainty principle vaguely, without attending to Heisenberg's idea that observation affects the object observed: this novel is a perfect illustration, in its action and its effect. The narrator's pursuit of his idea will make the guilty act innocent and the innocent look guilty, so how can he ever verify his hypothesis? He is the observer trapped in observation. There is a picture in the house, a strange pastel of a face and a mask, 'the picture, of all pictures, that most needs an interpreter' (ch. 4). The spectators disagree not only about the resemblance of the face and the mask to 'some face in our party' but about the picture's allegory – Death or Life – the mask's expression – grimace or smile – and its sex. It figures the narrator's curiosity, frustration, and materials, but also generalizes these things, and makes them more ambiguous and strange. The novel might have taken its title from the mask, but the mask is not erotic enough.

The sacred fount is the narrator's image of a secret source of sexual influence. Through his 'psychologic' reading (as Obert, the professional artist in the story, calls it in justification), he may detect the secret *ménages*. The key question is not crudely formulated as 'Who is sleeping with whom?', but this is what the narrator and his collaborators are asking. (The collaborators are under suspicion, so may lack detective detachment.) The sacred fount is one of James's most amusing sexual symbols, presiding with sly reverence over a story of prurient gossip, speculation, curiosity, and voyeurism. Its cunning lies in its mix of poetry and epistemology, with a hint of bedroom farce. No doubt this is why it has infuriated serious critics.

But there is that poetry. This odd story has a lyrical invocation of nature rare outside James's travel-writing. Urban and urbane artist that he is, James uses beautiful nature as sparingly as Jane Austen, preferring nature civilized and improved. Henrietta Stackpole calls herself 'deeply human' and the indulgent phrase fits this narrator, who needs indulgence more than Henrietta. As he goes in to the garden in hot pursuit of proof and people, he sees May Server, one of his objects, at the end of a vista. The mixed feeling of creative excitement and pitying tenderness is written into the natural setting. His feeling must not be romanticized, because pity does not check pursuit, as he recognizes he is 'trapping a bird or stalking a fawn'. His pastoral and romantic images are placed in a literary and painterly frame, with an emphasis on romantic imagination and shape-making:

> I had positively encountered nothing to compare with this since the days of fairy-tales and of the childish imagination of the impossible. *Then* I used to circle round enchanted castles, for then I moved in a world in which the strange 'came true'....
>
> My few steps brought me to a spot where another perspective crossed our own, so that they made together a verdurous circle with an evening sky above and great lengthening recesses in which the twilight thickened. Oh, it was quite sufficiently the castle of enchantment.... We were in a beautiful old picture, we were in a beautiful old tale. (ch. 8)

This aestheticism and structuralism prepare for his subsequent comments on extravagant perception and diffused glamour. The narrator is aware of his objectifying gaze – his observations and interpretations – but within the frame there is admiration, and pity for the woman's attrition. This is a sensibility making its inference: 'I saw as I had never seen before what consuming passion can make of this marked mortal on whom, with fixed beak and claws, it has settled as on a prey. She reminded me of a sponge wrung dry and with fine pores agape. Voided and scraped of everything, her shell was merely crushable' (ch. 8).

The shifting, bizarre, but precise images fix May Server and the narrator's emotion for her. The grotesque style of compassion is in character but pierces the humour and self-consciousness of the artist-narrator, making it clear that the story is not a mere joke, the teller not a mere voyeur, as well as establishing and justifying passion as his subject. He understands passion, as well as feeling it, when he says it moves us by something not ourself. The subject is his gaze, but he knows there is a subject beyond his gaze. The insight moves us out of the ironic play of self-parody to register perception, perhaps love. James offers his unsympathetic readership a self-parody which would mirror their distorting image, if they were clever enough to write it. Only it qualifies parody with moments of deep feeling. You do not really parody yourself.

*The Sacred Fount* is as moving as it is impudent, and a sentence from James's Introduction to *The Tempest* for Sidney Lee's 1907 edition of Shakespeare (*CM*, no. 55), explains why it is not a freak but a predecessor to the three novels which follow. Like Shakespeare's play, this strange novel 'seems to show us the artist consciously tasting of the first and rarest of his gifts, that of imaged creative expression....' He does so with irony, humour, fantasy, and gravity.

The second short novel of the late period, *The Outcry*, is James's last novel, based on his last play, which, like *The Saloon* and *The High Bid*, was written at the request of producers and actors – Charles Frohman, Allan Wade, J. M. Barrie, and Granville Barker. Deciding they did not want his adaptation of *The Other House*, they encouraged James to write *The Outcry*; he revised and cut, it proved difficult to cast, and it was finally doomed by the death of Edward VII, which closed the London theatres. It was produced eighteen months after his death, Shaw pronouncing its language unactable, its author ignorant of the *viva vox*, Granville Barker comparing its stylized dialogues to Restoration comedy. James turned it into his weakest novel. When a dramatized version of *The Aspern Papers* was produced and acted, with Michael Redgrave brilliant in the male lead, it thinned into nonentity by extroverting its first-person narrator. James's plays failed because they lack the filter of narrating consciousness. When James rewrites his play as a novel, he does not replace the loss of that sensitive register, at once subject and object, which is his imprint. So we have that freak, a Jamesian narrative without the central register.

The narrative in *The Outcry* is virtually restricted to stage directions. It expands the play, but still reads like a bald scenario. Even though it is a novel, it is much more behaviouristic and sketchy than the text of a Shaw play, for instance, with its dense observations on character, ideas, and history. James's slightly filled-out stage text simply appends to dialogue descriptions of conduct, motive, and emotion which would be shown in performance, as in the following examples: 'obviously tried to look neither elated nor snubbed . . .' (ch. 8), 'it appeared to take him time to read into these words their full sense' (ch. 1), and 'the explanation came after a brief intensity of thought' (ch. 8). There are occasional brief passages of more inward narrative, but they are scattered arbitrarily through the book, and instead of being part of the character's viewpoint are mere enlargements of description. The next sentence might come from almost any of the novels – *The Portrait of a Lady*, for instance, which uses garden-imagery to describe character – but there it would be part of a character's self-analysis and not a narrator's comment on a character: 'You might somehow have traced back the whole character so presented to an ideal privately invoked – that of his establishing in the formal garden of his suffered greatness such easy seats and short perspectives, such winding paths and natural-looking waters as would mercifully break up the scale' (ch. 6).

The novel is a thinly fleshed-out play, the stage directions not analytic, or generalized, or in free indirect style. The novel is not really a novel, and its neglect by James's critics is understandable. It simply reminds us of the important central consciousness which is not there. Its subjects of the art market, an acquisitive and pretentious culture, collection, and expertise, are precisely documented with names and prices, in the smart, satirical, witty, but unindividualized dialogue. The characters are undeveloped, the point laboured. There was contemporary interest in spotting allusions to Bernard Berenson and American collectors like Isabella Stewart Gardner, and the question of art values and exports is still alive. (There is a sharp comment on the Elgin marbles.) But unlike *The Awkward Age*, James's most dramatic novel, which amusingly imitates the dialogic form of drama but knows it is a novel, *The Outcry* is a fossil, perhaps of interest to art historians and students comparing plays with novels. It is a reminder of the brief period in the Edwardian decade when James was solicited by the theatre, and wrote plays which had very short runs or none. He worked hard at the plays, but took the experience calmly, not repeating the hope and disappointment of his earlier theatrical attempts.

# 4

# *The Ambassadors*

*The Ambassadors* (1903) begins James's new century. It did not come out until 1903, but he spent most of 1900 writing what he judged his best 'all round' work, the novel that seems closest to James himself, in its central character and its concern with solitude, renunciation, and two cultures. Unlike its successors, *The Wings of the Dove,* written in 1902, but published first, in 1902, and *The Golden Bowl,* written next and published in 1904, it is not a love-story. It is a *Bildungsroman* with a hero of middle age, Lambert Strether, the first and most important of the novel's ambassadors. Most of them, though not all, cross the Atlantic to convert the young Chad Newsome to the materialist and puritanical culture of New England. Like the ghost on the jolly corner, and most of James's key symbols, the idea of an ambassador is picked up from the surface of the novel, in casual references to ambassadors being the sort of people you might meet at Gloriani's reception.

Strether is one of James's most lovable characters, and perhaps the one most capable of loving, though we do not see him in love. It is arguable that in this novel nobody loves, with the possible exception of Madame de Vionnet, one of James's enigmatic characters. The international theme is conspicuous, containing a preoccupation begun in the first stories, then powerfully developed in *Roderick Hudson* and many of its successors. In *The Ambassadors* the contrast between Europeans and Americans is the vehicle for a scrutiny of the determined self. It anticipates the subject of 'The Jolly Corner' but is far from being a fable, adapting the classic *Bildungsroman*, the novel of maturation and growth, to tell one of fiction's most sustained and elaborated stories of the making of moral and affective life. It is about imagination, and a reflexive narrative.

Technically, it continues James's continued experiment with point of view, keeping close to a central consciousness, and restricting narrative voice to a small though important space between character and reader. The inventor of this minimal narrative was Jane Austen, the English novelist with whom James had most in common, whose genius he belittled in his lecture, 'The Lesson of Balzac', in patronizing figures of thrush and needlework. (He also speaks of her 'glory' as he lists the variety of novelistic talent at the end of 'The Art of Fiction' (*CM*, no. 26). James reinvented and gave a name to Austen's subdued narrator and centres of consciousness.

The narrator keeps so consistently close to Strether that the reader almost falls into the trap, earlier set by *Emma,* of identifying with the central consciousness, despite the scrupulous distance set between characters and narrator. The restraint of this authorial narrator and the concentration on the character's awareness are teasing. There are things we are uncertain about because the narrator does not support, contradict, or qualify what the characters say, think, and feel. One example is Strether's famous imperative 'Live!', his rejection of New England values (bk. v, ch. 1). We do not know if we should approve his advice to the young painter, Little Bilham, to live 'all he can', though most critics do, including Tony Tanner and Leon Edel. The recommendation is given in direct speech, at an early stage in the novel, at Gloriani's reception. After this scene many things happen to qualify Strether's excited advice to get what you can out of life without worrying about what you do as long as you do something. At the time of the speech, we have a sense of Strether's limited New England culture, and his significant savouring of simple sensuous pleasures in England and Paris. Little Bilham later varies the words, rendering 'live all you can' to 'see, while I've a chance, everything I can?' (bk. vi, ch. 3) which Edel reads as emphasizing the visual sense so strong in the Parisian culture. It is also a change, cunningly put as a question, which slightly unsettles Strether's uncompromising hedonism, with its echo of Pater's famous amoral injunction in *The Renaissance* to savour the moments as they pass. It is advice never repeated or retracted by Strether himself, even after encountering several people who seem to be living life to the full. What should we think of it?

We do not know whether to accept Strether's reason for returning to America and rejecting Maria Gostrey's offer of shelter and union. On the last page he says he must not 'have got' anything for himself 'out of the whole affair'. In a sense he has got all he can want, given Chad's imperfection and the undesirability of Woollett and Paris. He has found or intuited an ideal, however unrealized in relationships and communities, a set of values, however negative in articulation. Perhaps he has not learnt what is right, but he has learnt that some things are wrong – lying to a friend, and abandoning a lover. But knowing what he learns still leaves us uncertain about that advice to Little Bilham: 'It doesn't so much matter what you do in particular, so long as you have your life' (bk. V, ch. 2). It sounded all right at the time, but now Strether has encountered the dishonesties and treacheries of living a full life. Do we recall his words, to revise them ruefully, to feel them innocently voiced by a mood and an occasion, tributes to a summer garden in Paris? Are we wrong to want the narrative to review its own past? It is important that the advice was given to Little Bilham and not to Chad. Recognizing this admits the lack of absolutism in the advice: had the words been said to Chad, Strether would have had to revise them, as he judges and advises Chad with a full sense of responsibility.

The narrator's guiding voice tells some things, but not everything. It does not evaluate. It does not tell us how to evaluate. George Eliot, whose authorial voice did evaluate, would have qualified Strether's pro-life affirmation: 'Strether was to hear his rash commendation of life lived for its own sake as a jangling echo', or 'Strether never changed his opinion, though events were to test its firmness and his fortitude'. She might have modified the renunciation of Maria: 'How was it that in the background of his consciousness he felt a stirring of relief instead of the expected pang of self-sacrifice?'

In spite of gaps, which solicit a reader's response, the line of development is lucid. Strether's liberation from the smug prosperity, narrow morality, and cultural thinness of Woollett, Massachusetts, starts with the novel itself, as he rejoices in solitude and his countryman's absence, enjoys Chester's ambiguous historic charm, and reveals ripe expectations in his *récit de voyage* to Maria. The innocent London glamour of theatre and supper with Maria prepares him for the heady air of Paris, where his susceptibilities flourish as his ambassadorial zeal flags. But as he responds to the sensuality and the beauty of Paris, his attempts to make a moral story out of Chad's friendship with Madame de Vionnet and her daughter show a distaste for sexual licence, even when it has a civilizing influence. Even the traditionally sanctioned young man's affair with the older woman is more than he can take. He delights in accepting Little Bilham's short-lived lie about it being 'a virtuous affair', but in the end 'the lie in the affair', and Chad's infidelities of spirit and perversions of art, disgust him, not the fact of adultery. Indeed, he wants Chad to go on committing adultery. His moral sense has broken the stereotypes.

He learns to make up his own morality, finding himself, without smugness, too virtuous for Paris and too imaginative for Woollett. He knows what he has missed in youth, but accepts himself in middle age, a melancholy but undismayed man torn between two cultures, unable to relax in Europe or to marry in America. He makes developments and discoveries as an imaginative spectator, his experiences vicarious but impassioned, like those of Rowland Mallett in *Roderick Hudson*. More positively than Mallett, he finds himself through an *alter ego,* Chad Newsome, attractive and repulsive. Like Mallett and Brydon, Strether recognizes that his character is socially fractionalized.

His story is an encounter with potentiality, its virtues and faults. Sent to Europe as ambassador, he sees the weakness – dullness, conventionality, smugness, materialism – of the culture he represents. Excited by the difference of aesthetic and sensual warmth and ease in the European culture, he mistakes them for the good life, but finds it has weaknesses too. Neither culture can have anything for him, because he is the hero of a fable about cultural extremes, without a middle way. What he discovers is something few of fiction's heroes discover. In Strether, James is revising heroes of earlier *Bildungsromane,* like Wilhelm Meister, Tom Jones, and David Copperfield, and revising fiction's heroines too. They are defined and developed by their relations with men, friends, and mentors, and Strether is defined and developed by his relations with women. As James imagines the poles of Strether's moral conflict – Mrs Newsome and Madame de Vionnet in antithetical relation, with Maria Gostrey as guide and mentor – he revises an old form, making it habitable by a new person. James is a creator of dynamic form, unfolding action and character, and the various stages of Strether's awakening show the integration James wrote about in his much-quoted 'The Art of Fiction': 'What is character but the determination of incident? What is incident but the illustration of character? What is either a picture or a novel that is *not* of character? What else do we seek in it and find in it? It is an incident for a woman to stand up with her hand resting on a table.'

Each set of incidents individuates a different character. Unlike Isabel and Maggie, Strether moves erratically, going round about like Peer Gynt. Expecting a gross licentious Chad, ruined by a loose Frenchwoman and a raffish set of artists, he is surprised by a civilized man in a discreet, socially accepted relation with a cultivated though unfortunately married woman of the world. It is an incident and a mark of character when Strether first reads Chad through the façade of his house, admiring its proportions, its 'discreet' ornament, and the 'complexion of the stone a cold fair grey, warmed and polished a little by life' (bk. II, ch. 2). In James's scheme of total relevance, every detail is expressive, as the discreetly personifying language helps us to see. Strether himself does some overt symbol-making, as he compares 'The balcony, the distinguished front' to 'something that was up and up', placing 'the whole case... as by an admirable image, on a level ... he might reach'. His interpretation is wrong, but the muted symbolism in the free indirect style, in which narrator places the character's optimistic but also cautious imagination ('as by an admirable image') is right. Chad turns out to have a discreet and admirable façade, his cold, fair, grey stoniness to have been warmed and polished 'a little'.

Chad moves in artistic circles, but he is not an artist like Gloriani, another of the mentors or ambassadors. Gloriani says 'He has wonderful taste' (bk. VI, ch. 2), and the praise conflates his taste in pictures and women. In the end, it will be applied in the art of advertising. Chad is a dilettante, though Strether responds appreciatively to his accomplishments, charmed by the sophistication and good manners of the boy from back home, as he is by the tourist treats of dining, 'breakfasting', talking a little French, and going to Notre Dame. Nothing like Rowland Mallett's aesthetic response to Roderick's sculpture, only a generalized relaxation of Woollett *mores* in the light and warmth of Paris, with the help and hindrance of the mentors. Everyone contributes to the making of Strether.

Madame de Vionnet and Chad are not disinterested as they charm and plead, pull this way and that; Little Bilham has to lie; the deserted Waymarsh deserts; Gloriani, 'expert' in life and art, warns and tempts him to envy; Miss Barrace agrees that they 'run too much to mere eye' (bk. V, ch. 1). Maria Gostrey's discreet hint that Chad's mistress may be a more civilizing influence than Woollett imagines is misleading, and when it looks as if she will have to act in complicity with her old schoolfriend, and perhaps lie too, she absents herself. When the three gloriously comic Pococks turn up, grotesque ambassadors of their cultures, they speed up Strether's conversion.

His fractionalized or divided self grows into a wholeness as he responds to lies, truth, and appearances. Two events in particular show him revising and integrating impressions. The first is the famous pastoral scene when he is under the spell of French landscape and impressionist painting. James is punning on 'impressionism'. Strether is like Elizabeth Bennett, whose original novel was *First Impressions*, but his New England culture wears its impressionism with a difference. Impressionist painting, which Strether has seen in Boston and on his first trip to Paris, sought the brief and fleeting impression, freezing the changing scene, cutting off narrative context at the edge. Fine for painting, not so good for people. Strether once nearly bought a real Lambinet, but he must break the frames and forms of his impressionism, his fashionably constructed romanticism.

He catches the lovers in a boat on the river, rowing out of deliciously blurred impressionism into the uncomfortable close-up of realism. Distance has allowed him to make up his story out of impressions. Narrative and impressionist painting are merged by the free indirect style as he makes the story and the picture:

> What he saw was exactly the right thing.... It was suddenly as if these figures, or something like them, had been wanted in the picture.... For two very happy persons he found himself straightway taking them.... They knew how to do it, he vaguely felt – and it made them but the more idyllic, though at the very moment of the impression, as happened, their boat seemed to have begun to drift wide. (bk. XI, ch. 4)

The drifting-wide admirably fixes the broken impressionism, and the end of their affair, in another image with total relevance.

Strether has to accept that they are lovers, enjoying an illicit trip, making a desperate polite attempt to save face. The scene is a coalescence of incident and character, but it is a cruder device as well, one of James's determining coincidences – as crucial as it ever is in Hardy, whose coincidences have had a worse press. James's 'Fordham Castle' and 'The Tone of Time' turn on improbable coincidences, while plot and characters depend on Maggie's coincidental discovery of the golden bowl. Perhaps James gets away with it because his dense psychological analysis distracts our attention from plot-mechanics. It serves his pessimism less blatantly than Hardy's coincidences. And James grasps the nettle, daringly reflexive, 'it was as queer as fiction, as farce' and 'fiction and fable, *were*, inevitably, in the air', the latter pair of literary terms separated by only half a dozen lines from Strether's translation into blunt phrase, 'there had been simply a *lie* in the charming affair' (bk. XI, ch. 4). (This kind of literary reference is found in *The American* and *The Golden Bowl*, among other examples.) Brought by coincidence to face the lie, Strether breaks the frame, hardens the light, and peels off the blurry glamour of his impressionism. It is more than a change of perspective. It is a shift of genre.

James does not allow this event to be the sole influence on his hero, any more than he sends Isabel Archer home to Osmond without the back-up motivation of her promise to Pansy. Strether's distaste at the lie in the affair is followed at once by the discovery that Chad is faithless to love and art. His loss of faith in Chad becomes retrospective, his disapproval of adultery and lies disguised by compassion for Madame de Vionnet and fresh disapproval of Chad. Another Jamesian absence here: Chad does not say that he is going to leave her, but to say that he will not is a way of saying that he will. Strether has succeeded in his embassy after all, in spite of himself. Chad will make a better manufacturer and capitalist for that educative time in Paris, which puts polish on his hardness, and teaches him about art, and how to make friends and influence people.

James does not tell us what the Woollett factory manufactures. He does not tell us what Strether will go back to, though we are relieved to know he will not be marrying Mrs Newsome, an off-stage character as monumentally powerful and unattractive as the fable requires. He does not tell us what Madame de Vionnet has in mind in her confidences to Strether, which may suggest a subtext of solicitation, more muted than Maria Gostrey's. Unlike Maria, she has been put in a sensuous relation to him, and even as she confides her desolation she may be offering him an opening as Chad's successor. We cannot see this possibility through Strether's consciousness, because it lies outside the range of his New England innocence, not yet educated out of existence. When it was first put to me as a likely reading, by Gordon Haight, George Eliot's biographer, I rejected it as unjustified by the text, but I now think it a possible implication. If it is a subtext, it gives a greater depth to his renunciation. And Madame de Vionnet is an ambiguous creation, from whose point of view we are totally excluded. Her last words to Strether are 'I've wanted you too' (bk. XII, ch. 2). Her clothes and her possessions and her speech are works of art. She is described as a *femme du monde* on her first appearance in a garden. Like Claire de Cintré in *The American*, Christina Light in *Roderick Hudson*, and *The Princess Casamassima*, she has been sold into marriage.

Strether cannot see her as an unhappy but experienced woman with a sexual future after Chad. He sees her romantically, not as a woman betrayed by her lover but a tragic victim of revolution like Madame Roland. One of the cunning things about this novel of middle-aged development is its openness. Strether ends by seeing much more than he saw at first, but not everything. He is still seeing too much and too little. His character and imagination are building, not completed. He has been shown not as free, but as made by his environment, and that is about to change again as the novel ends. The ending is less closed than it appears.

In one way it does appear closed. In 'The Art of Fiction' James writes with gleeful scorn about the demand for a happy ending , a 'distribution at the last of prizes, pensions, husbands, wives, babies, millions, appended paragraphs, and cheerful remarks', and ending 'like that of a good dinner, a course of dessert and ices'. The author of this ending is not 'a sort of meddlesome doctor who forbids agreeable aftertastes', but he is a sort of doctor who risks a prognosis. Like Huck Finn and Gabriel Conroy, Strether turns westward, taking nothing for himself. In *The Appropriate Form* I suggested that his renunciation of Maria Gostrey's delicate offer 'of exquisite service, of lightened care, for the rest of his days' is redundant:

> He has revised both his first prejudices about the effects of Europe on Chad, and then his hasty romantic view of Chad's superior refinements. Having cast off two illusions he is left to make the renunciation of any personal advantage – except the advantage of knowledge – which the affair has brought him. But this last renunciation is made to appear strongly active, unlike his earlier reactions which have followed inevitably and more passively on seeing the facts. It is as if James were making the moral collocation... in *The Portrait of a Lady,* where Isabel makes a similar advance in moral perception and ends with the last fine development showing itself in a painful open-eyed disregard of self. (p. 42)

Isabel is personally involved in a way Strether is not, and his renunciation has something gratuitous about it: 'having learnt that there is coarseness in Woollett and betrayal in Paris, he cannot... accept the future Maria proffers' (p. 42). James says in the Preface that the last scene adds nothing, the relation projected has nothing to do with the matter and everything to do with the manner. This is hard to accept, because James is consistent in moral emphasis: Strether has learnt to see, and to see the defects of his seeing. He has seen Chad as a might-have-been young self, more creative, sensual, bold, and civilized. (There are references to Chad's earlier Parisian adventures.) His admiration is voiced in the scene where he advises Little Bilham to live, immediately before Strether feels a sexual envy for Gloriani, a famous womanizer, 'I know... whom *I* should enjoy being like!' (bk. V, ch. 2). By the end it is clear that Chad is not an acceptable might-have-been and we never know if Strether still envies Gloriani.

The New York millionaire is not acceptable to the Europeanized Brydon: *The Ambassadors* is an anticipation of 'The Jolly Corner', the story a revision of the novel. Had the young Strether stayed in Paris and not settled down to cultural mediocrity and editing in Massachusetts, he might have read all those lemon-covered books, bought a Lambinet, learnt to speak better French, lied, brought up a son, not been widowed, had love affairs, committed adultery, gone into advertising, and made a million. There is a reciprocal pattern here too, and my list of possibilities suggests a reason for James's seemingly artificial conclusion. I no longer feel so sure that the renunciations of the two Marys is gratuitous.

If Strether has seen both extremes – Parisian and Woollett, the dilettante and the manufacturer – as undesirable though understandable historical constructions, renunciation is a good ending. He takes nothing for himself because he is suspended between two selves. Brydon can accept Alice – his Maria Gostrey, but properly beloved – because she has helped him to see the rejected self as a possible self, who cannot be wholly discarded. If we read the novel in this way, it makes better artistic sense of the ending. It may also explain why James changed his mind about making Strether a novelist and made him a mere editor, known because he is editor of the journal, not editor because he is known. His cultural marginality and his lack of creativity place him with Chad, not Gloriani.

We cannot know James's intentions in the advice scene, based on words spoken by W. D. Howells to Jonathan Sturges in Whistler's garden in Paris and recorded by James in his notebooks, 'Live all you can...' (*Life*, ii. 414), so should probably read the speech neither as a rash simplification nor as advice for all sorts and all seasons, but as locally understandable and making sense if prudently interpreted. It seems likely that the imprudence expresses Strether's mood rather than his final opinion, but that is the most we can say. As Leon Edel comments, when James used the words 'he would pay attention to the line "live all you can", and not to another phrase noted down "I'm old. It's too late"' (*Life*, ii. 209). He revised the words carefully, and left them in the air.

To stress these structural complexities is not to ignore the realization of Strether's character as warm, generous, self-effacing, and imaginative. He is not an exclusive and engrossing 'I', but he is central and equipped for centrality by his responsiveness. Like Mrs Dalloway's, his back goes up in the presence of other characters, relations, images, and symbols. He must not be identified with his author: in those reminiscences of youth to Walpole, James looks back on his past as lived, not unlived. The relationship between Strether and Maria Gostrey may derive from James's close friendship with the novelist Constance Fenimore Woolson, whose violent death greatly distressed him, and who is usually identified with May Bartram of 'The Beast in the Jungle', and Strether's susceptible but isolated celibacy would be congenial to James. But though Strether is susceptible, he is not an artist, or he would have left Paris with a great deal 'for himself' like James.

Like all James's central characters, Strether is what James spoke of in *Notes of a Son and a Brother* as 'a man of imagination'. Like the woman clerk 'In the Cage', Owen Wingrave, Spencer Brydon, Maisie, Fleda, and all the major figures in the fiction, he is equipped for the task of hero and chief narrator. He is fractionalized, by his two cultures, but capable of shifting the parts around. He is a wonderfully alert and analytic companion, self-conscious but sensuous, savouring light and warmth, sensing temperament and character, changing his mind with humour, chagrin, and fortitude. As he interprets, we interpret his interpreting mind and senses. He is equipped to make the scene, in Gloriani's garden, by the river, or watching the women in Notre Dame. When he takes Madame de Vionnet out to lunch on a sunny day in Paris for the quintessential romantic French *déjeuner*, it is a scene whose particulars have become famous, more like a Bonnard than a Lambinet. The grey-eyed woman with her elbows on the white linen, the tomato salad, and the straw-coloured Chablis are significant items in Strether's paradise and sensuous gifts for readers. It is a novel which needs to be sensuous, because it is about a sensuous man enjoying Paris, but its rich tactile and painterly rendering of colours, textures, and tastes is a poetry delightful in itself.

# 5

# *The Wings of the Dove*

Like *The Ambassadors* and *The Golden Bowl,* this middle novel has a presiding symbol announced in its title, and makes its symbolism internally, through the characters' creative effort. There are several capable of inventive and transformative ways with words: Kate Croy, Merton Densher, and Milly Theale are filters of consciousness through which we see the events and people of the novel. They are made to make the language which is medium and subject.

The imagery and lexis of the opening chapter are totally relevant to the novel: the heroine's self-inspection in the mirror, her divided gaze, beauty, and mourning, the squalor and small size of room and street, family deaths, dialogue between father and daughter, everything tells. The scene sets an environment, placing and motivating Kate's improvised scheming. She is a case of visible social shaping, determined to be a villain, in one of Richard III's meanings: not intending to be a villain, she adapts to soliciting circumstance. Like Christina Light and Marie de Vionnet, she is made by beauty and poverty into commodity. The power of market value is backed by persuasive circumstance – a friend in need, possessed of all the wealth Kate and her lover Merton Densher lack and want, dying to love before she dies.

When we put the novel down, Densher's acquiescence in Kate's plot may seem implausible, but on the page we slip with him, step-by-step, through the soliciting circumstances which encourage desire, submissions, then renunciation and change. The process is gradual, almost imperceptible, though towards the end not always crystal clear, as it moves from his complicity to his anger at Lord Mark. It is unmistakable in conclusion, as he refuses to take the bequest with the woman for whose sake he wanted the bequest.

This novel builds in blocks, dividing analytic narration between characters who create the terms in which action and judgement are articulated. Milly is the dove, in innocence, whiteness, softness, purity, spirituality, and flights of love and death. There is her well-known prototype, in James's young cousin Mary (Minny) Temple, who died of consumption at the age of 24, thirty years before he wrote the novel. The letters he wrote after her death and twenty years later, as he hatched ideas for the novel, show how he appropriated her vitality and doom, but the novel is not autobiographical. (Alfred Habegger's criticism of James's revised version of Minny is discussed by Philip Horne, who also deals intelligently with the question of Minny's appropriation in the novels.) Milly is not Minny, even if she derives from her sickness and life-longing. Like that little domestic object made in Woollett, her illness is not identified. Like all the gaps and absences in James, it is a habitual withholding of information, and functional in its particular context. (Here it is perhaps also a fastidious distaste for a Dickensian pathology of faints, gasps, pants, and coughs.) Kate says Milly will not smell of medicine and her dying occurs off stage, creating suspense for reader and characters, and signalling a solitude in suffering. But in the central sections of the novel she is one of James's most creative characters.

Milly's absence at the end is functional, like her late entry on a stage already peopled by the *dramatis personae* of Poverty, Dependence, Love, and the Match-Maker. We meet her enigmatic in the black and white of pallor and mourning, after we have met Kate, a sympathetic character who is also enigmatic: apparent moral laxities, like clandestine correspondence and a secret engagement, are sometimes deceptive, sometimes not. Kate proposes honest or selfless actions which would foreclose the potentials of the plot: to live with her father and give up her aunt's protection. She engages herself to Densher 'for ever' in one of those rushes of passion not infrequent in James, but rare enough to be startling. This novel needs to be passionate, since sexual desire – and kinds of love – motivate the characters. The two first meetings of Kate and Densher, in a private view and a tube train, are wonderful scenes of mutual attraction, followed by collusive dialogue, the tension before touch, then the embrace and kiss. When we meet Milly, and Susan teases her awkward reticence about Densher, we know she hasn't a chance. Narrative irony and emotional representation go hand in hand.

If anyone believes James cannot do passion, they should reread the scene in Venice after Kate has been to bed with Densher and he is left with the aftermath. James used indirection, suggestion, understatement, and sustained metaphor to show passion, in Yeats's words, by battening it down and letting us feel the stirring of the beast beneath: 'when, with each return, he worked his heavy old key in the lock. The door had but to open for him to be with it again and for it to be all there; so intensively there, that, as we say, no other act was possible to him than the renewed act, almost the hallucination, of intimacy' (bk. IX, ch. 1).

The avoidance of explicitness in the repeated 'it' and the repeated 'act', the tiny move from the unspecifying pronoun to the more specific but common 'act', with the careful qualification of that 'almost' – this is memory, not hallucination – show nuance and scruple at work. In a characteristic freshening of stale metaphor, the 'act' takes us into imagery of a repeated run at the theatre, helped by the repeated dead and revived metaphor of 'view':

> Wherever he looked or sat or stood, to whatever aspect he gave for the instant the advantage, it was in view as nothing of the moment, nothing begotten of time or of change could be, or ever would; it was in view as, when the curtain has risen, the play on the stage is in view, night after night, for the fiddlers. He remained thus, in his own theatre, in his single person, perpetual orchestra to the ordered drama, the confirmed 'run'; playing low and slow, moreover, in the regular way, for the situations of most importance. (bk. IX, ch. 1)

There is economy in this micro-narrative of imagery, reanimation of metaphors, and the logic with which the metaphor of the fiddler's audience blends into the image of Densher as orchestra, rather than spectator. The world 'own' in 'his own theatre' has powerful resonance.

In this passage, absolutely necessary in the portrayal of passion as motive, Densher is shown as passive, in the grip of memory and obsession. John Goode, in *The Air of Reality*, finds the passage voyeuristic and neurotic, and I can only register a different response, finding a powerfully rendered generalization about sexual memory particularized for this novel. (Kenneth Graham also praises the narrative as a vehicle for sexual feeling.) Sexual memory is by definition passive, but passivity is appropriate at this time, in which Densher is shown as fixed, first by his promise to Kate, then by his exclusion from Milly. The passiveness is also part of the moral portrait of an imaginative man with a capacity for corruption and a capacity for change. He is rendered passive by his desire, unsatisfied and briefly satisfied, for Kate. Finally, his passiveness is a retreat from moral seduction, a good neutrality.

Densher is a journalist of the social and international scene, like his author, and his skill at imaginative analysis is energized in Maud Lowder's 'vast drawing-room' (bk. II, ch. 2), as he interprets space and objects, knowing like Madame Merle that things are expressive. James shows him as perceptive rather than inventive, 'the message of her massive, florid furniture' and 'the immense expression of her signs and symbols' received rather than projected, but by a writer who turns reading into writing: 'He read more vividly, more critically . . . the appearances about him. . . . It was the language of the house itself that spoke to him. . .'. And as he finds a word for this 'writing out' of 'the ideals and possibilities of the mistress', he reflects writer-like on the word: 'He was glad to have found this last name . . . "cruel" somehow played into the subject for an article – an article that his impression put straight into his mind'. Like Jane Austen's descriptions, James's work dramatically, through the impressions articulated by character. The process is dynamic: in the act of finding a language for impressions he realizes how he is at the mercy of the Lowder philistinism and ugliness, how powerful they are, how 'These things finally represented for him a portentous negation of his own world of thought' (bk. II, ch. 2). This is James's imaginative register of character, through which the data external to individual mind are presented as public and private event.

Densher's creative perception creates more symbols at the end, when he has been excluded from Milly's dying presence. The weather and inhabitants of Venice are made physically substantial and symbolic: cold lashing rain and wicked raging wind are jarring and wrong; his exiled and wretched state is imaged in the stranded and wageless people. Symbols expand – the ruin of grace and beauty is reflected in the wet and slippery piazza, symbol of European social life and Renaissance culture, 'a great drawing-room, the drawing-room of Europe, profaned and bewildered by some reverse of fortune' (bk. IX, ch. 2). Densher's change of heart, his alienation from Kate and his attachment to Milly, are all confirmed. His symbolic perception is more than creative reading – it is the index of a new moral sensibility.

Kate Croy's creative reading is evident from that beginning, where an elegant free indirect style merges authorial analysis with characterized sensibility. In later scenes her sensibility becomes inventive, initiating the symbolism of the dove. There are one or two premonitory images of flight, for instance, at Mrs Lowder's dinner-party, where Milly – 'our young lady' – is said by the narrator to alight and wave her wings (bk. IV, ch. 1), but the flight-and-bird image is made specific by Kate as she tells Milly, 'you're a dove' (bk. V, ch. 6). The creation of this symbol works rather like Brydon's creation of his ghost – it gets out of hand. Kate seems unaware that she is handling a symbol with sacred connotations, and these connotations appear at the end of the novel, where Milly's power, to change and attach Densher, makes the conclusion. When Kate's love and her plot are overwhelmed by Milly's appropriation, it is the solution of a long conflict of images.

Early on there is a transference from Kate to Milly which anticipates the ending. Milly's interpretation goes beyond Kate's. First she thinks, '*That* was what was the matter with her. She was a dove. Oh *wasn't* she?' (bk. V, ch. 6). This is enigmatic, but Milly's independent handling of the image begins as she compares the indulgent conversation of Kate and Mrs Stringham to 'dove cooing to dove', then tells Mrs Lowder about Densher's return, in words she thinks are 'the most dovelike', which means 'earnest' and 'candid' but also crafty. She is putting on a dovelike act, which makes her feel 'the success she could have as a dove'. She works at the part, 'she studied again the dovelike' and 'She should have to be clear as to how a dove would act' (bk. V, ch. 6). The last intention is clearly cunning, describing her plan for diverting Sir Luke Strett to Susan Shepherd Stringham. At one stroke James makes it plain that Milly is no soft gentle peaceful dove and no passive recipient of image-making. To be converted into metaphor is as reifying as to be framed by the gaze of camera or canvas, and James's perception of creative power includes the perception of such reductiveness. Milly's perception, resistance, and appropriation of the image foreshadow Kate's failure and Milly's moral victory. The reduction to image, in a less than wholly imaginative act of image-making, is something of which the recipient is made fully aware. James is showing two women engaged in a power struggle, and the simplifications and appropriations of rhetoric – originally the science of linguistic power in law court and market-place – are dramatized and exposed.

It is not just a matter of language, but also of action. Kate makes Milly the object of her image-making as a preliminary to manipulating her illness and life-longing, in the way in which James manipulates his functional characters who belong to the manner, not the matter. Milly is not made to resent being called a dove, but her elaborations and variations on Kate's metaphor anticipate her bequest to Densher, which makes her the manipulator. The title becomes knowing and ironic as the novel proceeds, and the attempts to appropriate it for Christian iconography are partial. But the title is more than ironic. Milly's flight goes beyond the range of Kate's metaphor, which becomes more mechanical but also less apt in Milly's reception in Venice, when Kate says, 'She's a dove... and one somehow doesn't think of doves as bejewelled', as she gazes at Milly's magnificent pearls, observed by Densher, who qualifies her image in the conversationally dynamic way of the late prose, in 'dim' glimmerings of his own future flights:

> Milly was indeed a dove; this was the figure, though it most applied to her spirit. But he knew that Kate was just now, for reasons hidden from him, exceptionally under the impression of that element of wealth in her which was a power, which was a great power, and which was dove-like only so far as one remembered that doves have wings and wondrous flights, have them as well as tender tints and soft sounds. It even came to him dimly that such wings could in a given case – *had*, truly, in the case with which he was concerned – spread themselves for protection. (bk. VIII, ch. 3)

Later on James makes his dove spread her wings, as Densher imagines, for protection, but also, as he does not imagine, to escape pain, terrors, and horror, as in Psalm 55:

> My heart is sore pained within me: and the terrors of death are fallen upon me. Fearfulness and trembling are come upon me, and horror hath overwhelmed me. And I said, Oh that I had wings like a dove! for then would I fly away...

The psalm fills in the gap occupied by Milly's pain, fear of dying, horror at betrayal and loss of love. Psalm 68 is also relevant, in its simile of a dove whose wings are 'covered with silver, and her feathers with yellow gold'. The withdrawn point of view is the more powerful because her imagination has been shown not only in the dove-images but in image-narratives of death. These are developed after Sir Luke Strett tells her to live, in a way which makes it clear she is soon going to die. James is a wonderful chronicler of place, and his novels show the descriptive powers of the travel books, which summon up a bridge in Venice, an old empty house in Les Baux, a corner of Washington Square, and a park in Dijon. In the novels his sense of place is internalized, made expressive of character: 'What is incident but the illustration of character?' he asked in his important essay 'The Art of Fiction' (*CM*, no. 26). Incident is made external and internal.

Milly is given the benefit of James's loving knowledge of London, after she leaves the doctor to go home on foot and ruminate on her mortality in Regent's Park. The doctor's words ring in her ears as she walks, pondering his instruction 'to live'. It is a vivid London scene, and a dynamic piece of symbol-making. Once more, the character makes the symbolic readings which dramatize her emotions, character, and predicament:

> she had come out... at the Regent's Park, round which, on two or three occasions with Kate Croy, her public chariot had solemnly rolled. But she went into it further now; this was the real thing; the real thing was to be quite away from the pompous roads, well within the centre and on the stretches of shabby grass. Here were benches and smutty sheep; here were idle lads at games of ball, with their cries mild in the thick air; here were wanderers, anxious and tired like herself; here doubtless were hundreds of others just in the same box. Their box, their great common anxiety, what was it, in this grim breathing-space, but the practical question of life? They could live if they would; that is, like herself, they had been told so; she saw them all about her, on seats, digesting the information, recognising again... the blessed old truth that they would live if they could. All she thus shared with them made her wish to sit in their company; which she so far did that she looked for a bench that was empty, eschewing a still emptier chair that she saw hard by and for which she would have paid, with superiority, a fee. (bk. v, ch. 4)

This is one of the great park poems, like Auden's 'Easter, 1929' and Dylan Thomas's 'The Hunchback in the Park', like them juxtaposing creative solitude and a publically abject poverty. With pathos and realism James marshals the familiar world of lovers, down-and-outs, children, animals, the whole battered urban pastoral, to animate Milly's recognition of Death the leveller.

Her vision is the ancient truth of classless mortality. James gives a twist to the ironic pastoral by imagining Milly's wealth dissolve when she sees herself as part of the poverty of ordinary London life. The scene is totally relevant to feeling and events, each word and phrase charged with her creative sensibility, reviving cliché and dead metaphor: 'the real thing', 'she went into it further', 'within the centre', 'the same box', 'the question of life', and 'breathing-space'. James breathes on the commonplace to light fresh meanings, always through an individualized mind – here Milly's dread-strengthened imagination. One of the best touches is the assimilation of a doctor's good but conventional opinion that the patient can live if she will, to the political opinion voiced in James's time, and all around us in our own, that the poor can live if they only will. Sensible to the hollowness of the precept, for sickness and poverty, he makes Milly and the poor strangers assimilate and adapt it to the knowledge that of course they would live if they could. It is a brilliant example of James's linguistic sensitivity and his political irony. His poor little rich girl is not idealized. Through the rich ambiguity of language she pities the sufferers, moving outside herself, through a pity for self which prompts insight. The scene is conducted by Milly's sick obsession with her sickness, a reasonable and reasoning obsession, like Lear's.

Her reflections on the compassionately oblique prognosis – wonderfully done by James in an act of medical stereotyping which stays particular – run through the scene. Her compassion for herself and for the down-and-outs all round on the shabby grass, is related to her doctor's felt compassion for her, which she feels as reductive. Pity is kept from being romantic by the experience of what it is to be diagnosed and pitied, to be a patient: 'he dressed out for her the compassion he so signally permitted himself to waste; but its operation for herself was as directly divesting, denuding, exposing. It reduced her to her ultimate state, which was that of a poor girl' (bk. v, ch. 4).

James daringly takes the dead metaphor 'poor' back to its origin, flaunting the obvious to justify and externalize Milly's self-obsession as introspective but not insensitive:

> that of a poor girl – with her rent to pay for example – staring before her in a great city. Milly had her rent to pay, her rent for her future; everything else but how to meet it fell away from her in pieces, in

> tatters. This was the sensation the great man had doubtless not purposed. Well, she must go home, like the poor girl, and see. There might after all be ways; the poor girl too would be thinking.... She looked about her again, on her feet, at her scattered, melancholy comrades – some of them so melancholy as to be down on their stomachs in the grass, turned away, ignoring, burrowing; she saw once more, with them, those two faces of the question between which there was so little to choose for inspiration. It was perhaps superficially more striking that one could live if one would; but it was more appealing, insinuating, irresistible in short, that one would live if one could. (bk. v, ch. 4)

Just as Milly revises Kate's appreciation of her soft and gentle dove likeness, she enlarges the doctor's pity and advice. It is by such acts of imagination that we read those absent responses to the knowledge that she has not been loved but used. James had written such humiliating knowledge into his *Portrait of a Lady* and here he leaves it unsaid and unseen after developing his character's independent creativity, a model for reading her suffering in his most writerly (*scriptible*) of novels. Milly is a tragic victim, but with powers. Densher's rumination in the piazza significantly emphasizes 'power... great power' and we first see her as powerful because of wealth but come to see her as powerful in deprivation. She does become a poor girl in a great city and does find there are 'after all... ways'.

James's villains, as well as his heroine, are victims. Milly's riches doom her, and their desire for riches dooms them. James shows how the corruption of love and goodwill is slow and gradual, as events and people play into Kate's increasingly opportunistic hands. From the occasion when she manages things so that Densher drives out with Milly, to the last sexual transaction in Venice, we see the decline of her courage, spontaneity of passion, and delight in his mind, and his admiration of her. The move from free vitality to a controlled and artificial language and behaviour is like Gwendolen Harleth's loss of spirit and fun after her marriage to Grandcourt. Here we see a relationship corrupted, a waste and destruction of a rare loving affinity, and the takeover of love by transaction and blackmail. The tragic loss is one for the lovers too, as true and truthful love is compromised and lost by false play.

The most puzzling member of the creative triad is Merton

Densher, not so much because his succumbing is implausible, as Tony Tanner says (in his *Henry James*) but because of the handling of his change of heart. This change is confirmed by one of James's functional characters, Susan Shepherd Stringham, a successfully particularized agent. When she tells Densher about the revelations which make Milly turn her face to the wall, there is an uncomfortable dialogue full of characteristically pregnant pauses and telepathy, a conversation in every sense, in which Susan's assumptions that he must be on Milly's side bring him over. Despite the simplifications in theological readings (for example, Dorothea Krook's in *The Ordeal of Consciousness in Henry James*), there is no doubt that the novel relies on a Christian ethic, like *Macbeth* and *Othello*. Densher is a Catholic, whose visit to the Brompton Oratory at Christmas after Milly's death strongly suggests that he is a penitent sinner, but though Milly is his redeemer, she is too particularized as American heiress and tragic victim to be a Christ figure. Susan Shepherd Stringham is also reduced and dehumanized by being read as Christ, but there is a touch of the good shepherd about her, shown most effectively in her thoroughly Jamesian telepathic expectations of Densher. Christian theology is present, but it is a novel which works as a humanist text also, old and new moralities coinciding as Densher meets a new self-image in Susan's humane faith. The corruptibility of love and relationship, and the historical construction of their corruption, are more complex and touching than religious readings suggest. But the moral processes are not always clear.

There is a certain glossing-over of Densher's conduct to Milly. The condemnation of Lord Mark comes more acceptably from Susan than from him. Mark is cruel and stupid in telling Milly about the attachment of Kate and Densher, but Densher's judgement is strikingly unaccompanied by self-blame.

There is a passivity in his relation to both women. His commitment to Kate's plan is a kind of acquiescence. After she leaves Venice, he knows, as she says, 'to stay *is* to try' (bk. VIII, ch. 3). Bound to Kate by 'the beauty of their own last passage' (bk. IX, ch. 1), he is grateful to Milly for not forcing him to choose between lying to her and breaking the pact with Kate. He does not like lying, and feels Milly's 'mercy' in not asking questions which will force it. The lie he does tell her is less difficult than the one he fears, though it is a serious lie for a writer, about writing: asked if he is beginning his book, he hedges, saying he has 'tried to think a few days ago', that he has 'broken ground'. After this evasion he begins to change, as if lying forced him towards truth. The transitional stage is characteristic of James in its use of symbolic place: Densher suddenly drops his objection to having Milly come as a guest to his rooms: 'His great scruple suddenly broke, giving way to something inordinately strange, something of a nature to become clear to him only when he had left her' (bk. IX, ch. 1). There is the ceding of Kate's territory, with the tacit end of his sexual possession, 'the drop, almost with violence, of everything but a sense of her own reality'. Since the lovers are treating Milly as an object, it is a crucial shift, but at the end of the chapter he is still on neutral ground, silent when pressed to say why he is staying, accepting Milly's 'because you've got to', and asking evasively if it 'isn't . . . enough . . . to stay after all for you?' She answers that he must judge. A move towards Milly is followed by a move back: he feels he is not disloyal to Kate but 'staying so little "for" Milly' that he is 'staying positively against her' (bk. IX, ch. 1), then after this swing back to neutrality he acknowledges 'her deep dependence on him' (bk. IX, ch. 2): 'Anything he should do, or shouldn't would have close reference to her life, which was thus absolutely in his hands – and ought never to have reference to anything else.' He admits that he still is not quite committed to feeling it, but reads it 'in the cards' (bk. IX, ch. 2).

He lives 'from day to day, and from hand to mouth' (bk. IX, ch. 2), until at the end of a precisely counted period of twenty days Milly stops receiving, and he moves into isolation, waiting for her death. It is during this time that Susan shepherds him towards Milly. He has been ripening towards virtue, or at least towards breaking the pact. During this slow hesitation Densher's conscience is dramatized so obliquely that we may search for its stirring. But it is not until later that we feel its absence, when he comes to condemn somebody else. The reader's dissatisfaction – not every reader may feel it – acknowledges the air of reality which makes James's reflexive characters also appear as moral beings. The novel's flaw is evidence of its strenuous effort to make treachery and acquisitiveness human, socially intelligible, not monstrous.

Densher demonstrates his change of heart, and though there is still no self-reproach there is no need for it. It is present in what happens. The rejection of marriage with Kate on her terms, and his rejection of Milly's bequest, is a conclusive moral act. The famous line 'We shall never be again as we were' articulates the loss of their virtue and the loss of their love, which Kate laments as she recognizes that he is 'in love' with Milly's 'memory', her conventional words for his developed sense of Milly's 'reality', which she reads as from far off. When he offered marriage 'as they were', it may look as if Densher is bargaining again with Kate, but there is no question of his terms being accepted and the transactions of love are repudiated, as they are in *King Lear*, unromantically. The novel knows and shows that they were comprehensible.

# 6

# *The Golden Bowl*

Perhaps there is a flaw in the next novel, *The Golden Bowl,* a novel about a flaw in a work of art. Once again a man shifts from one woman to another, and moral and psychological significance is imputed to the move. Books rewrite their successors, and *The Golden Bowl* revises the triangle of Milly, Kate, and Densher, turning its power-and-love story into a four-sided shape. Amerigo, the prince, is won by his wife, Maggie, from his mistress, Charlotte, and the victory involves much condemnation of Charlotte and some condemnation of the man. There is a strong moral sense in the novel which emanates as explicit utterance from Maggie herself, though also from implications of the action. In *The Appropriate Form* I argued that, like *The Ambassadors,* this novel showed a protrusion of the structural sense within the characters. James might wish us to see Strether gain nothing from his successful and unsuccessful embassy, but it is hard to take the renunciation of a relationship we never feel as an object of his desire. Readers of *The Golden Bowl* may conclude that Charlotte helps to make the union of Maggie and Amerigo, but Maggie's gracious sentence 'It is as if we had needed her . . . to build us up' (bk. VI, ch. 2) would come more sensitively from the narrator – or Fanny Assingham, since James's narrator does not draw such conclusions. At times the characters show the strain of their narrator's reticence.

Maggie's is a moral tit-for-tat, like Milly's bequest, which ensures posthumous victory over Kate. But Milly dies, which makes her victory less smug. Novels often revise romantic cliché. *Wuthering Heights* is about love being 'too big' to resist, *The Wings of the Dove* about being in love with a memory, *The Golden Bowl* about wives and husbands who don't understand each other. When the wife who doesn't understand comes into her understanding and her marriage, we don't rejoice – or, if we do, we don't simply rejoice – at the victory for marriage but at the victory for a liberating imagination. Maggie puts herself in Charlotte's position, that of the powerful manipulating the less powerful, acting on behalf of the people she loves most, as we all do, except saints. She also acts on her own behalf, as a person initiating actions and taking charge, big moves for a little woman and mere wife. The Prince and Charlotte refuse to lose the world for love, try to have the world and love too, and are punished by the world, fixed in their conventional worldly roles of married womanizer and society beauty and hostess.

Charlotte makes Maggie into a manageable object, and the Prince leaves her when he begins to see Maggie as a person in her own right, which is not until she sees herself. By strenuous imagination, Maggie sees her loss, retrieves the husband she has never had, and achieves a measure of liberation, more subversive than it looks at first sight.

She begins with herself, feeling herself manipulated, but also acts on behalf of her father. He is a character whose imagination might preside and there is enough sense of structural reversibility to propose that the novel could be told from his point of view. His withdrawn viewpoint makes him enigmatic, like the Master in the ambiguous 'Lesson of the Master'. His reasons for marrying and for leaving at the end are different from Maggie's, but we infer that he may be using quietist methods to save her, as she saves him. There are moments pregnant with this sense of reversibility, as she imagines her father's imagining. They are like two people expecting each other's appearance round a corner they approach but do not turn: 'She held her breath, for she knew by his eyes, the light at the heart of which he couldn't blind, that he was, by his intention, making sure – sure whether or no her certainty was like his' (bk. V, ch. 3).

The reversible structure is clearer because the novel establishes a rotating view. As 'The Prince' is told from the point of view of a narrator close to the Prince, looking over his shoulder – and 'The Princess' does the same for the Princess – there is a moral implication in the narrative engagements. The Prince perceives as long as he retains the power to perceive, but loses narrative dominance as he loses power to the self-liberating Maggie, who grows into her narrative engrossment, as James suggests in the

Preface: 'The Prince, in the first half of the book, virtually sees and knows and makes out everything that concerns us – very nearly (though he doesn't speak in the first person) after the fashion of other reporters and critics of other situations.'

Maggie takes over when she starts seeing, and the Prince loses centrality and does not see what is going on. His exclusion, like Densher's, is a nemesis designed for a dominant male. The woman's dominance is gained by artful passive-seeming moves, a pacifist politics. Both the woman and the man attain some measure of liberation from their conventional gender-roles.

Charlotte is never allowed narrative occupation, but the Prince, destined for liberation, is granted it for a while. It is a moral structure: Charlotte is too sexually self-concerned to be the register of action, Maggie is at first unqualified for narrative centrality, Adam is suggestively and ambiguously reserved, so Amerigo first takes the position, *faute de mieux,* showing a promising openness in seeing and in what he sees. The narrative chorus of the happily married Assinghams is justified by wit, commitment, detachment, and intimacy. They are knowing and not knowing, a Lockwood and a Nelly Dean in conversation, childless observers of a family drama, active in their small unstable social circle and gossiping for dear life.

In the first paragraph the novelist creates character and scene, preparing the narrative future. The Prince is delicately established as a womanizer, as he does not care for possibilities in women's faces:

> The young man's movement, however, betrayed no consistency of attention – not even, for that matter, when one of his arrests had proceeded from possibilities in faces shaded, as they passed him on the pavement, by huge beribboned hats, or more delicately tinted still under the tense silk of parasols held at perverse angles in waiting victorias. (bk. I, ch. 1)

In 'shaded', 'tense', and 'perverse' there is a gathering suggestiveness. In the second paragraph imagery is more emphatic: the settling of the marriage had 'something of the grimness of a crunched key in the strongest lock that could be made' and 'It was already as if he were married, so definitely had the solicitors, at three o'clock, enabled the date to be fixed.' As James says in the Preface to *The Tragic Muse,* the novelist's art, like the dramatist's, is the art of preparations.

The beginning is the symbolic title. The novel's central image derives from a 'real' object, the gilded cracked crystal bowl found in an antique shop in Bloomsbury, first by Amerigo and Charlotte, then by Maggie. Like the dove, the bowl belongs to texts and traditions: to Ecclesiastes ('Or ever the silver cord be loosed, or the golden bowl be broken'), the Grail legends, and Blake's Thel, whose motto asks 'Can Wisdom be put in a silver rod or Love in a Golden Bowl?' There are cup and bowl symbols in George Eliot's *Romola*, and in James's previous work – Roderick Hudson's statue of a drinking boy, Madame Merle's cracked cup in *The Portrait of a Lady*, and the role of a Veronese cupholder proposed by Susan Shepherd for Densher. Images of drinking deep and draining the cup of life are commonplace. The novel's symbolism is sociological too. There is an obvious offence against the rules of donation in proposing a wedding present with a crack, as the Prince's Italian superstitiousness, 'Per Bacco!' confirms (bk. I, ch. 6). And the bowl is a sexual symbol in a novel about the dangers and wonders of sex.

The bowl is animated, almost a character, with a destiny which takes a turn in the second book, where it also gathers new meanings. Maggie buys it as a present for her father, and at a high price which does not arouse suspicion of a flaw, then is enlightened by the contrite antique-dealer who sees family photographs and tells his tale. She sees the bowl broken by Fanny Assingham, explains the breakage to Amerigo, and stands the pieces together again on her mantelpiece. Fanny uses a sympathetic magic to show the crack in Maggie's idea, benignly reinterpreting the symbol. Tony Tanner says Maggie smashes the bowl (*Henry James*), but she does not, and could not, because she is not a destroyer but a restorer. The law of total relevance holds.

The symbolism works through the characters' awareness, as with the dove, but the bowl is present as a specific object. The familiar doves that flutter round St Mark's are unspecific, hidden in the scene. The bowl has charm, sensuous presence, and a history. Its entry is elaborately delayed, like that of a character in drama, as the dealer turns to 'a receptacle', unlocks it, extracts a 'square box, of some twenty inches in height, covered with worn-looking leather', puts the box on the counter, undoes the hooks, and removes 'from its nest a drinking-vessel larger than a common cup, yet not of exorbitant size, and formed, to appearance, either of old fine gold or of some material once richly gilt' (bk. I, ch. 6). He handles it 'with tenderness' and 'with ceremony', makes a place for it 'on a small satin mat', and introduces it. '"My Golden Bowl",' he observed – and it sounded on his lips as if it said everything.' It is made personal by the introduction and the warning which accompanies it: 'As formed of solid gold it was impressive; it seemed indeed to warn off the prudent admirer' (bk. I, ch. 6).

Though the scenario for the novel does not mention the bowl, it is involved in relationship, action and values. Physically present, unlike the abstracted dove, it is implicated like the dove in the feeling of its fiction, essential to plot and an image of value. Like all the late writing, including the revisions, the novel has a baroque imagery, in narration and idiolect. In 'The Lesson of the Master' Paul Overt is told that his characters all speak alike. James's characters do not, but they are alike in rhetorical fertility.

As Charlotte seductively plays with the central symbol – like Kate with the dove – comparing the summer day of lies and adultery to a great gold cup she and Amerigo will drain, she forgets the cracked bowl she nearly bought so cheap for Maggie, and is oblivious of pious resonance. The bowl, like the dove, is a sacred object, and Charlotte, like Kate, tempts Providence by secular selection. The traditions are against her. Blake asks if a golden bowl can hold love, Ecclesiastes reminds us that it is breakable, the Grail legend knows it is holy and attained by subduing the flesh. When Maggie dreams of the bowl without a crack, as it was to have been, she is open to larger meanings, though her's is an erotic, as well as a hallowed, quest.

At the beginning of her own book, Maggie sits feeling displaced in her own drawing-room. Like Densher's scruples about entertaining Milly where he and Kate have made love, her sense of strangeness is significant. James's imaginative characters are alive to the poetics of space as they inhabit houses, rooms, and furniture. James stages the interaction of Maggie's inner drama and physical environment, as he did with Isabel Archer's vigil in her drawing-room, after seeing her husband seated while Madame Merle stood. The social psychology of space is understood by James's characters, as territorial as cats. The drawing-room is a place Maggie uses, after becoming aware that she is being used. What can only be imagined by the reader about Milly Theale's last responses is explicated for Maggie, to whom we are as close as to Strether.

First she uses rhetoric of building and space, imaging a hypothesis as 'some strange tall tower of ivory' (bk. IV, ch. 1), refining and revising by trial and error, 'some wonderful beautiful but outlandish pagoda, a structure plated with hard bright porcelain, coloured and figured and adorned . . .'. The image figures mystery, alien occupation of 'the garden of her life', enforced action (she has to walk round it), then restriction of space and impenetrability (it has no door). It suggests interiority: when she knocks there is an answer, 'a sound sufficiently suggesting that her approach had been noted'. The exotic doorless pagoda is succeeded by an ordinary door made strange.

Maggie seats herself in the room as an act of conspicuous change, because her husband will expect to find her in her father's house. She compares her suppressed vague worries to 'a roomful of confused objects, never as yet "sorted"'. The image grows from simile to metaphor, expanding space: 'like a roomful' becomes a room, with corridor outside and a door, and imaginative Maggie as imaginary character, sometimes passing the door, sometimes turning its key to 'throw in a fresh contribution'. Scene and action become more complicated and objects more animated, then confusion gives way to clarity: 'it was as if they found their place. . . . They knew where to go.' The 'as if' keeps the image-story provisional, then, as the fantasist gazes at her own image gazing at the jumbled and unjumbling heap of things, the imagined open door through which she is looking gives way, in a startling shift of imagistic and narrative register, to the 'real' door of her drawing-room: 'the sight of the mass of vain things . . . made her in fact, with a vague gasp, turn away, and what had further determined this was the final sharp extinction of the inward scene by the outward. The quite different door had opened and her husband was there' (bk. IV, ch. 1).

Once we learn how to read James's prose, it is fluid and dynamic, full of surprise. For reader as for character there is a stair missed in the dark. James shows how the 'outward scene' is converted into conceits and narratives of the 'inward scene', but makes imagination cope with real doors as well as imaginary ones. He works through daring juxtaposition. Maggie has to turn from her startlingly animated imaginary objects in imaginary rooms, to use imagination on real people and real objects in real rooms. She experiences a frightening shift from imagination to reality, and from subject to object. We share the character's shifts and shocks, experiencing an intimate closeness to them, while at the same time the shifts in rhetorical register keep us in touch with the fact of fiction. We are reminded that the 'real' drawing-room door and the man who comes through it are also figments and figures – the shift of plane accentuates fictionality. James is the most writerly of novelists: we have to work in order to read, and read as his characters read, provisionally and vaguely as well as definitely and precisely, working through a complex text in which one imaginative construction exists inside another, like a Chinese puzzle, which is also a work of art carved in ivory.

*The Golden Bowl* is a love-story with a kind of happy ending. One couple is reconciled, in desire, parenthood, and imaginative affinity. The other physically sterile couple leaves to establish the Verver Museum in American City. The novel ends with an embrace as Amerigo tells Maggie he sees only her. It is an affirmation of change and home-coming, a symmetrical return to his first averted gaze. Maggie has gained what she wants, Amerigo's total desire and a control of her own desire, the golden bowl as it was to have been. A fascinating strand of the story is Amerigo's attempt to control Maggie by his love-making. She is afraid of her own desire, and when she is playing for time, patiently, actively, silently, she keeps him at a distance, not to punish him but to keep her head. Amerigo and Maggie, as well as Amerigo and Charlotte, are a passionate couple. James's sexual suggestiveness is powerful in that scene when Maggie surprises Amerigo by the ordinary act of waiting for her husband in their drawing-room. She wants to go upstairs with him while he changes – in desire or trial – and behind his joking refusal is unwillingness to go to bed with his wife so soon after going to bed with his mistress in the Gloucester inn. It is a wonderfully rendered moment of domestic awkwardness, like the lie in the affair when Strether meets the lovers. James is a keen student of the social problems of illicit love, and in the drawing-room scene nothing is made explicit, everything suggested.

In these three novels, James knowingly and originally dramatizes sexual desire, sexual memory, sexual dependence, and sexual corruption. When he uses understatement or suggestion, his reticence, like George Eliot's and Thackeray's, carries a sexual charge which was probably felt the more powerfully at a time in the English and American novel when sexual explicitness was unknown, except for pornography. His reticence is precise, not vague, and the implied powers of physical love are important in this novel because Maggie's growth in sexual knowledge and control is a part of her liberation. She learns to resist being manipulated by her Italian husband's experienced love-making, as she comes to know how he uses it. The Prince, in his turn, is a wonderfully ironic study of a man's passive acquiescence in his constructed role. Charlotte's seduction of him is made possible because she plays on his sexual power and pride, subtly taunting him with Maggie's preference for filiality, offering herself in ways not resistible by such a man in such circumstances. The social expectations are intricately present at the house-party where Amerigo and Charlotte linger to keep their hostess and her man company, and there is a fine sense of *louche* complicity, not wholly enjoyed by the Prince.

The withdrawals and the waitings for a sexual union, as part of the reconciliation, contribute to that sense of elated affinity which makes the happy ending. *The Golden Bowl* is James's *Liaisons Dangereuses*, in which the cynical womanizer finds that the virtuous woman – no less victim for being wife – resists becoming his love-object. Laclos's novel imagines a rake trapped in sexual pride, complicity, and conquest, incapable of love though able to reject his mistress-accomplice, and James rewrote it for his time and culture.

In spite of Maggie's and Amerigo's measure of liberation and growth, *The Golden Bowl* troubles readers because of its ambiguities and silences. Doubt is incident to readings of such indirect narrative, where there is no authentic, or authentic-sounding, interpretation or opinion, but this novel bristles with questions. Does James sufficiently condemn Adam's possessive paternity and Maggie's filiality? In spite of Maggie's realization that husband must be put before father, we know Adam feels more for child and grandchild than for wife. Does James sufficiently condemn the power of capital? Charlotte and Amerigo, like Densher and Kate, are motivated by a distaste for what is only relative poverty, though wealth is presented as a source of love's corruptibility. Within his social and economic parameters, James is condemning acquisitiveness and the cash nexus. Is he designing too facile a victory for marriage and the family?

There is a problem of power, perhaps more apparent at this stage of feminist consciousness. In the scene where Maggie looks through a window to see her husband, her father, and her mother-in-law at the bridge table – everything is relevant, including bridge – she feels responsible, knowing, and powerful. As with the nameless narrator of *The Sacred Fount* and Strether by the river, she is placed as fiction, at her moment of vision, by a reflexive literary reminder, as she looks at the bridge players through the window and thinks they could be actors rehearsing a play 'of which she herself was the author'. This is one of several literary reflections which emphasize her fictionality and her fictionalized power. That power is presented as painful responsibility, though her self-image as scapegoat has a touch of complacency, like the final placing of Charlotte which smacks unpleasantly of an ex-lover's dismissal and a married woman's smugness. Maggie pities Charlotte when she hears her 'high coerced quaver' before the cabinets in the gallery (bk. V, ch. 4), lies when asked by Charlotte if she has worked against her marriage, and finally asks, 'Isn't she too splendid?' (bk. VI, ch. 3). She defeats deceit by deceit, illicit relationship by institutionally privileged relationship, and cleverness by imaginative superiority. She is humiliatingly used, and in her turn manipulates, while saving her victim's face. It is important to see her process as one of liberation, but like other liberations, it causes damage. Just as wealth corrupts love and imagination, so of course does power, and Maggie loses as she gains. She patronizes her rival as her rival has patronized her. It is a move in the balance of power, first in Charlotte's hands then in Maggie's. There is a fascinating irony in the increasingly passive role of the Prince, so conventionally masculine and aristocratic at the start, but pushed into an ancillary place as a consequence of breaking his role. It may look like woman against woman, backed by an unpalatable married complicity, but Maggie and her husband have moved away from degrading acquiescence in socially constructed gender roles. He is no longer the humiliatingly conventional rake, she no longer the complacent little woman married for her fortune. James is not writing Utopias but novels, and though the relationships are illustrative, they are earthed by social likelihood. Maggie's liberation involves Charlotte's constriction.

Charlotte offends against sisterhood in her adultery, her marriage, and the belittling of her friend, but the sense of a biter bit is barbaric, the struggle discredited. It is a war – like many – in which the victor achieves the position of the vanquished. Maggie achieves more than this, because it is satisfying to see people grow up, and hers is a woman's dearly purchased power. If it is a flaw in the novel James thought his most perfect, it is because gender-history has gone beyond it. Virginia Woolf imagined the problems for women of achieving a man's power, while James showed the achievement as a happy solution to problems, insufficiently politicizing his characters' developments. To put it another way, Maggie and Amerigo lend themselves to a modern anti-sexist interpretation, within limits. But the novel should be welcomed, I believe, because of James's ability to show a man's gender-restriction, and his measure of subversion, as well as a woman's, which he had been studying since *The Portrait of a Lady.*

James and his creatures are bounded by the social imagination of late-Victorian and Edwardian England and New England. They could scarcely have been revolutionaries in their place, class, and time. James unconsciously articulates the dilemma of socialists and feminists who cannot see a way to defeat patriarchal capitalism, so adopt its tactics, fight with its weapons, and hope for victory on its terms. A contemporary James could extricate the women in his novel from their marriages, and endow them with a more radical liberating urge and achievement. To put the novel back into its history is not to condone James's attitudes to women and sexual competition, only to observe that he failed to see beyond the conventional support of wife against mistress, but does not condemn Amerigo and Charlotte so much for adultery as for mercenariness, deceit, and manipulation.

Here too 'everything is terrible in the heart of man', and in spite of another Catholic backdrop, the flawed human heart is not monstrous but visibly misshaped. Even Charlotte, selling her sexuality and beauty, patronized by lover and rival, forcibly repatriated, denied issue, lowered by lies and excluded by silence, is allowed to survive becoming a commodity, to make a career. She is a spirited wrongdoer like Kate, showing a brave brinkmanship as she offers to show the Prince's telegram to Verver before they marry, the plot hanging by a hair's breadth. It is a reminder of the fullness of the person being fractionalized, and one of the images of contingency which make James's socially illustrative novels more than fables.

# 7

# The Unfinished Novels: *The Sense of the Past* and *The Ivory Tower*

Two unfinished novels represent an extraordinary might-have-been. For *The Sense of the Past* we have nearly three hundred short pages, of the New York Edition, with another seventy pages of James's ruminative scenario for the completed novel. He began writing it early in 1900. Leon Edel refers its origin to a railway journey with Kipling's publisher F. N. Doubleday after lunch with the Kiplings, and their discussion of another volume of ghost stories. James 'seemed to see, as the train sped him back to London, "the picture of three or four 'scared' and slightly modern American figures", against European backgrounds... "hurried by their fate... in search of, in flight from, something or other... a quasi-grotesque Europeo-American situation"' (*Life*, ii. 343–4). Out of this came the scenario for Ralph Pendrel's story, with the title *The Sense of the Past*. He started this in January, continued in the summer, then laid it aside to work on Strether's search and flight, also for something and from something. He tried again in 1914, continuing the narrative from the chapter in which Ralph tells his time-travel story to the American Ambassador and enters his house and the past, went on for 180 pages, then dictated the scenario, with its development and ending. Edel guesses at problems with the ambitious time-travelling fantasy, and dissatisfaction because of the war, but Percy Lubbock's note to the New York Edition tells us that James went back to the novel after difficulties with *The Ivory Tower*, interrupted it to write his introduction to Rupert Brooke's *Letters from America*, and was about to resume when he had the first stroke in December 1915.

The subject was difficult and ambitious, and James had no use for the historical novel because he knew it was impossible to reproduce past language, but there seems no reason to suppose that he would not have finished it, in view of the full scenario in which problems are articulated and solved as he projects narrative and analyses projection, quoting *'solvitur ambulando'*. We have a novel which is about one-third written, with about two-thirds in the form of speculative, problem-solving summary and discussion – a wonderfully mixed and readable discourse which blends with the formal part of the novel because it is narrative as well as analytic and because the novel is reflexive.

It anticipates 'The Jolly Corner', which may not have been written without this first story about doubles and destinies. Ralph's journey is from America to London, where he discovers an American double living ninety years before him, with a passion for seeing the future conveniently equal to his own historian's passion for seeing – and smelling, touching, and tasting – the past. The two change places, and Ralph enters into a complicated destiny, worked out in the scenario with tact and logic, in which he has to repeat his other self's life, trying to avoid anachronistic deviations. The point about recurrence and variation which is a problem for science-fiction stories is dealt with briefly and intelligently, and James's story takes its placed with his friend and rival H. G. Wells's earlier *The Time Machine* as a progenitor of the subgenre. Like all James's ghost stories it has the solidity of specification he valued and a thoroughgoing dramatized motivation for fantasy. His supernatural always appears utterly natural, and it is worked out with rational consistency and psychological depth.

The love-story naturalizes fantasy: Aurora, Ralph's twentieth-century beloved, longs for a man of action, and his time-adventure is a quest performed for her. James probably named her after Tiresias' beloved, for whom he risks a normal existence in time, though the mythical dimension is disguised by her distaste for the Old World. Ralph is involved with two women in the early nineteenth-century past, and one of them, Nan, rescues him by a subtle sacrifice. (Not in the narrative but worked out in the scenario.) Like 'The Jolly Corner', this story has a collocation of imaginative adventure and desire, a fearful and novel ordeal. The story is another attempt to test historical conditions: the hero is a writer trying to imagine the past, against the odds, and the author of his experimental journey tries with admirable strictness to imagine a modern man living the life of a nineteenth-century ancestor. The story uncovers differences of two regions and two times, as it quietly considers historical conditioning: 'What shall we call the self?' James's story is full of fascinating details about language, money, and even dental technology – these last reflecting James's trips to the dentist as a child and elderly man. It is about history.

It is about imagination. Ralph anticipates Brydon's creative fiat when he imagines the old house as a laboratory for the historian. James's ghost-seers are always motivated, like Julius Caesar, Hamlet, and Macbeth, and through Ralph's keen mind James shapes apparitions from the past, using his hero's courage and historical obsession as form and fiat. Like the girl 'In the Cage', Ralph is a medium. James uses a picture to frame his vision, one of many paintings which, like his cages, doors, and windows, are images of entrance, boundary, selection, and threshold. In this novel James speaks of a frame as a threshold. Like the golden bowl and Brydon's stranger, the painting and the past self are given a ceremonious introduction as Ralph slowly proceeds through three rooms to be checked on the brink of disclosure by the portrait of a man's back. As he ponders the strange pose he spins a 'fine thread' like James in his preamble and plans. He tries different hypotheses, to end with the wild fancy that the painted subject turns his back '*within* the picture', 'when one's step drew near', otherwise looking 'as figures in portraits inveterately look'. Ralph's imagination is said to take 'a monstrous jump' and conceive 'a prodigy'. This jump is a creative speculation: if the figure can turn its back, will it show its face? Like Lewis Carroll and Cocteau in *Orphée*, James uses a magic mirror, because, when the figure turns round, it is to show Ralph himself, *Doppelgänger* not *alter ego*. So the fantasy begins, within the will and art of the character.

*The Ivory Tower* is a successor to *The Golden Bowl*, with a dominant symbol in title and book. It was begun in 1913, and given up when the war began. Like the bowl, the tower is not mentioned in James's notes. It may derive from the pagoda in the previous novel, but it is a miniature, a carved ivory cabinet into which the hero puts an unopened letter. It also recalls the painted triptych in

*Romola* into which Tito shuts away a cross. The image might have expanded to express a desired and undesired isolation from the world of 'ferocious acquisitiveness', as James called the American money-making scene. Both heir and heiress, Graham Fielder and the massive Rosanna Gaw, hate their riches, each with a certain inconsistency, since she persuades Graham's stepfather to leave him wealth, and he does not refuse the bequest. James's plans were well developed for a story of money, corruption, manipulation, treachery, and renunciation, rewriting characters and situations from *The Portrait of a Lady, Washington Square, The Wings of the Dove,* and *The Golden Bowl,* in a New England setting. There are sketches of an American version of the Lowder vulgar money culture, and striking characters, like Rosanna and the detached Graham, but since relationships are barely begun, the lengthily analytic dialogue is not clearly characterized. Still, as a bitter comedy of manners it makes a start, and is backed and completed by James's notes for the whole novel, enlivened by some of his strongest rejections of the corrupting and corruptible money culture.

# 8

# Late Tales

When Richard Garnett made a selection of James's short fiction, he preferred the 1890s, choosing few tales from the earlier and later periods. The late stories, as is often said, are harsh and bitter, though one of the best, 'The Jolly Corner', resolves harshness in harmony. It was no accident that led T. S. Eliot in *The Family Reunion* to locate his Orestes' vision of the Eumenides in a not 'very jolly corner' as he saw his predecessor converting furies to angels of justice.

Some late stories after 1904 are anti-American, but not destructive. They reel under the shock of that famous return journey, but continue the themes, forms, and feelings of James's work in the genre throughout his career. 'Crapy Cornelia' is routinely quoted for its attack on the decline of modern manners, vulgarity, and the money culture, but its returned native finds a sacred archive, presided over by Cornelia's presence, and there is certainly no unrelieved cynicism. There are stories which shine out. 'The Beast in the Jungle' takes the idea of the unacted life, compressing complex characters, enigmatic dialogue, and symbolism to unfold suddenly in James's introverted but startling denouement. Like 'The Jolly Corner', itself a recall of earlier ghost stories, this marvellously titled story harks back to other tales of the unfulfilled life, like 'The Altar of the Dead', where James, who perhaps chose perfection of the work over perfection of the life, imagined alternative responses to celibacy and solitude. The story is not directly autobiographical: James is isolating one aspect of self-interpretation, and the central figures, though 'men of imagination', are not artists. 'The Beast in the Jungle' risks the symbol of a wild animal, making it stand for an agonized discovery, in imaginative retrospect, of lost opportunity for passion. The quiet understated narrative justifies the bold choice.

Here we feel Yeats's beast stirring.

The short stories run into each other, used by James as a fluid medium, like his novel scenarios, in which he imagines different endings to one story. 'The Jolly Corner' reimagines not only the exile's character and history, but the tragic love-story of John Marcher and May Bartram, reborn as Spencer Brydon and Alice Staverton, another couple who share deep secrets but who face the beast inside the self together. The stories complement and illuminate each other's language. In 'The Jolly Corner' we have fantasy developing from narrative to metaphor and back to narrative, and 'The Beast of the Jungle' shows the same generative process, placed within character and creating reflexive fiction, in a realistic action. Metaphor in title and personal language-set brings realism to the threshold of fantastic incarnation. Like Brydon, Marcher conceives the story's symbol, and the story in it, in a visibly self-generative process. When May retells his story to him, she speaks of 'the deepest thing' within him, 'the sense of being kept for something rare and strange, something prodigious . . . that would perhaps overwhelm' him. He hits on the beast-image after their acquaintance becomes friendship, and he rejects a thought of marriage because 'a man of feeling didn't cause himself to be accompanied by a lady on a tiger-hunt'. The last image harks back to the previous sentence, 'Something or other lay in wait . . . like a crouching beast in the jungle.' The writer makes it clear that the imagistic bestiary is Marcher's: 'Such was the image under which he had ended by figuring his life.' The irony is perfect – the beast is released by a lack of passion, an over-civilized self-engrossed thinking on the event. Realization of his loss and responsibility comes with a violent spring, as Marcher sees in another man's 'raw glare' of grief what 'passion meant', and in the same stroke, his own lack, and the meaning of his image: 'It was the truth, vivid and monstrous.' The image carries passionate horror for the unacted life but it also fulfils his prediction that he will recognize the beast in retrospect: 'It had sprung in that twilight of the cold April when, pale, ill, wasted, but all beautiful, and perhaps even then recoverable, she had risen from her chair to stand before him and let him imaginably guess. It had sprung as he didn't guess; it had sprung as she hopelessly turned from him.' Like James Joyce's 'The Dead', the story ends with a man seeing his incapacity for love but valuing the seeing in a recognition appropriate to the artist, who may not always experience at first hand but can perceive losses with intensity.

Other stories of the period include the sharp comedy of 'The Birthplace', and the fantasy of 'The Great Good Place', the one transforming our visits to Stratford, the other a religious fable and a beautiful funny dream of repose for the work-weary, with a richly strange thank you to good secretaries. The comic sense complicates and refines social satire in 'Fordham Castle' and 'Julia Bride', and the ferocious story of sexual revenge, 'The Two Faces', in which a discarded mistress seizes her opportunity and demonstrates James's capacity for passionate understatement. Edel is right about James's freshly uninhibited treatment of revenge in some stories, but most are emotionally complex, like 'The Abasement of the Northmores', bitter about literary reputation but delighting in the marriage of true minds. I would disagree with Edel's emphatic judgement that these late tales express James's disenchantment.

Like the novels, they create an affective trajectory which cannot be summed up by simple naming of the passions. Some of his happiest love-stories are here, mingling bitterness with a tender celebration of human strengths. 'The Velvet Glove', said to have been written in response to Edith Wharton's request that James should introduce a volume of her work, is spiteful, but 'The Papers', an amusing, tender, and satirical story about an appealing couple of journalists and the power of the press, and 'The Tree of Knowledge', about the happy family life of a bad sculptor, are comic and serious, affectionate and evaluative, crammed with social observations and psychological subtleties. Deriving from a writer's experience, wry and jealous, but exultantly knowing and amused, they make up the promised 'picture of my time'.

They are well-plotted stories of the imaginative life, packed with surprises. In 'The Beldonald Holbein' a society beauty takes a back seat, for unusual reasons, and taste for looks and art is exposed with glee. In 'The Story in It', James shows a Wordsworthian sense of finding a story where the insensitive observer would find none. One of his best stories of love and marriage, 'The Bench of Desolation', whose title inspired an image in W. H. Auden's poem 'As He Is', tells the moving history of a weak second-hand book-dealer and a strong woman who threatens him with breach of promise. These tales are surprising, witty, richly metaphorical, animated in dialogue, making the reader work for pleasure and enlightenment.

# 9

# Travel and Autobiography

James was a fine travel writer, and in his late period continued writing about Italy and France, but in 1907 published *The American Scene*, which he liked to think of as the best of its genre. The European essays addressed the uninformed, but the American book is for the travelled and the untravelled. He had written about America before, essays on Saratoga and Newport in 1870, and Niagara in 1871, but these are occasional pieces. His writings on France and Italy, though working well as books, were collections of journalistic essays, but the new book was conceived as a new genre of traveller's autobiography. It belongs to a small subgenre, the narrative of *nostos*, the return journey. It records marked social and demographic changes, becoming history as well as geography and topography. It is a blend of memoir with travel-essay, though as memoir it is reticent, cutting out the names of friends, companions, and hosts. It is a tribute to James's physical energy and alertness as a traveller at 61. It is one of his unfinished books, as he projected a sequel which was never written, for which notes survive. It has had interesting editors, including W. H. Auden. It has been criticized for political incorrectness, chiefly in the descriptions and anecdotes of Jews and blacks.

Auden says James is not a journalist but an artist, for whom travel is the most difficult subject because it deprives him of 'freedom to invent', that 'successfully to extract importance from historical personal events without ever departing from them, free only to select and never to modify or to add, calls for imagination of a very high order'. Perhaps Auden exaggerates inventiveness as a novelist's gift not shared by the poet. In the Italian essays, for instance, mostly written in the 1870s but collected in 1901 as *Italian Hours*, James is happy not to invent but to criticize and appreciate, and offers fine discriminated response to Italian art, Venetian and Florentine painting in particular, and sensuous descriptions of landscape and architecture. In language he is always inventive, his impressions made amusing and personal. It is a pity that Auden's praise of this most remarkable travel-book is made at the expense of the excellent essays in which James writes simply and directly, in his most laid-back style, poking fun, for example, at Ruskin's dogmatism, so different from his own relaxed and open responses.

Auden calls *The American Scene* James's most ambitious work of topography, 'a prose poem of the first order', describing the style as 'modern Gongorism', and showing how conceits and personifications work amusingly to displace description and create a dialogue between seer and scene. The animated apostrophizing of buildings, railway, the Past, the Muse of History, and the American woman, by the critical and nostalgic 'restless analyst', as James calls himself, makes lively reading, but it is found in the earlier essays too, and here it compounds the book's generalizing habit, which makes it often less specific and less scenic than the earlier European essays. It is more socially analytic and speculative than the earlier travel-writing, but the conservative bias of its generalization becomes predictable. James is constantly wincing away from people and things. He could not stand skyscrapers, did not admire Chicago, and his likening of the Manhattan skyline to a broken comb reminds us of Alice Staverton's idea in 'The Jolly Corner' that Spencer Brydon might have invented the skyscraper. It is the story of a conservative's return to a homeland and a scene which had changed remarkably over his twenty years of exile, and much of the response seems closed to a modern sensibility, though Auden found James's judgements of American manners and education congenial to his own conservative middle age. Of course the rejections and snobberies must be seen in their time, of their time. His tour of the New York ghetto was conducted by a Jewish friend and host, but his language grates on a modern ear: 'There is no swarming like that of Israel when once Israel has got a start, and the scene here bristled, at every step, with the signs and sounds immitigable, unmistakable, of a Jewry that had burst all bounds' ('The New York Ghetto', *AS*, no. 4).

It recalls the patronizing and stereotyping tone when Adam

Verver buys Damascene tiles from a Jewish family in Brighton. We should not be surprised that James complains about negroes being bad servants, putting too much sugar in his coffee and dumping his bag in the mud, and must set these personal criticisms in the large political context of his anti-racist observations on Southerners. His stories of a first visit to the South, an old enemy made newly visible, are astutely and entirely Northern in their antipathy to slavery and their astonishment that the South could have imagined secession as politically viable, and their dismay at the aftermath of the Civil War, for blacks and whites. There is the often-quoted meeting with a gallant young Virginian, who casually boasts of his father's 'lucky smashing of the skull of a Union soldier' and whose readiness to fight the cause over again leaves James to wonder about his political consciousness, 'till it came to me that, though he wouldn't have hurt a Northern fly, there were things (ah, we had touched on some of these!) that, all fair, engaging, smiling, as he stood there, he would have done to a Southern negro', ('The Young Virginian', *AS*, no. 12).

James is consistently writing as a Northerner (as in *Notes of a Son and a Brother*, where he evokes *Uncle Tom's Cabin* as powerful story and stage-play, and the happy childhood of relatives who grew up to fight and die in the Civil War). Here he animates a defeated South whose 'spirit' is imprisoned in 'the haunting consciousness of the negro'. He uses the individualizing personification which delights Auden to image the attrition of the Southern conscience:

> It came to one, soon enough, by all the voices of the air, that the negro had always been, and could absolutely not fail to be, intensely 'on the nerves' of the South, and that as, in the other time, the observer from without had always, as a tribute to this truth, to read the scene on tiptoe, so even yet, in presence of the immitigable fact, a like discretion is imposed on him.... The moral... became... a... dirge over the eternal 'false position' of the afflicted South – condemned as she was to institutions, condemned to a state of temper, of exasperation and depression, a horrid heritage. ('The Burden of the South', *AS*, no. 12)

The feminine personification and tiptoeing jerks of syntax are evasive as well as expressive of James's response, articulating James's awareness of a continuing Southern problem, not all that far removed from Faulkner's picture in *Intruder in the Dust*. And it is directly related to James's detailed social observations, as when he deplores 'the maintenance of a tone, the historic "high tone", in an excruciating posture' ('The Epic Dimness', *AS*, no. 12).

James's own tone is not always as considered as it is in these sections, and of course the modern reader can feel critically superior as well as amused when fastidious James records the horrors of hotel children, young extrovert noisy fellow-travellers, and Italian immigrants lacking the charm of the Italian in his native Italy. James is not naïve; he knows, in that last instance, that he is observing first-generation European immigrants whose children will become Americans, and his fear for the future is a fear of a levelling and a standardizing of national identity. He sometimes sounds like a modern anti-federalist Tory looking apprehensively towards the new Europe, but dramatizing his dread analytically and wittily. What makes this book hang together, and still readable, is its mingling of humour and melancholy for historical elegy and autobiography as well as travel-book.

This chord, sounded softly or harshly, is found again in the stories, the autobiographies proper, and the biography, *William Wetmore Story and his Friends* (1903), a book written in two months, in response to the family's request. Described by James as a making of champagne from small beer, it is more of a lament for the artist life of Rome in the 1870s than a biography. Its charm lies in its acts of memory – James was at the age when the backward glance was becoming congenial. He was hampered, though not too much, by a low opinion of Story's sculpture, which he describes as prosperously pretentious, making it sound more like the work of the phony Morgan Mallow in 'The Tree of Knowledge' than the art of Roderick Hudson, which in other ways it seems to resemble. As Story's milieu had been his own, he recalls it to contemplate the life of an American exile, speaking of the expatriate's problems, and, with tactful gentleness, of his old acquaintance's lack of concentration and single-mindedness. The book evoked a famous response from Henry Adams, who told James it was his story, and the story of a whole generation of bourgeois Bostonians, including Emerson, Longfellow, Lowell, and James, kept ignorant and shallow 'by Harvard College and Unitarianism', all 'improvised Europeans... and – Lord God – how thin!' (*Life*, ii. 491–2). Adams's lament recalls the story of Strether rather than Henry James, who had become Europeanized, and aware, not ignorant, of the historical shaping of his career.

The richest personal narrative is James's three-volume unfinished autobiography, begun after William's death in 1910, which left him feeling mutilated by an 'extinction' which changed 'the face of life' (*Life*, ii. 725). Returning from his last American visit to Rye, then London, he began dictating his brother's story. It was soon taken over by his own childhood memoir and became *A Small Boy and Others*. Published in 1914, it is a personal story which joins social, cultural, political history, and family anecdote. A little later he wrote a sequel, *Notes of a Son and a Brother*, dealing with his own 'obscure hurt', the Civil War, his brief Law studies at Harvard, and family portraits, then began a third volume, posthumously published in 1917 as *The Middle Years* and little more than a fragment. The autobiographies are lavish with anecdote and character – Thackeray joking with the children, Emerson's visits, the unTennysonian Tennyson, Lewes and George Eliot coping with Thornton Lewes's mortal illness and on a later occasion rudely returning James's work, with tales of a huge extended family, including the 'cousinship' of which many were orphans, and others doomed to die of tuberculosis and war.

Although these memoirs are histories of the author's artistic growth, they also tell the story of a family, with a central strong and loving portrait of his father, Henry James Senior, the generous free spirit careless of convention, money, and self, imaginatively bestowing on his children the cosmopolitan cultures and liberty from which at least two of the boys, William and Henry, profited. Like John B. Yeats, who also saw the freedom he gave his children flower to genius, the elder James was a liberal father, conventionally married to a woman felt by husband and children to be an ideal wife and mother, a woman of her time, totally absorbed in family and marriage. The younger brothers, Wilky and Robertson, emerge as characters through their war experiences, told in family letters made part of the narrative. Alice, the subdued gifted woman, is remembered tenderly, but stays in the shadows. Too rich to summarize, this 'niggling tapestry', with its dropped threads, weaves a public and private story, in a rambling, digressive form, mixing discourses, and strikingly different from the economical shapely fictions. James finds a form for the chronicle of a family, and of an artist's developing consciousness in the culture of two continents.

The autobiographer is nothing if not purposive as he sees in the small boy's inner life and outer pleasures the beginnings of his art, and his warm memory of early response is the chronicle's charm. For example, recalling early visits to the Louvre, on a first visit to Paris in 1855, on the courier's arm, he contemplates the fertilizing effects of the education their examination-and-mark-hating father offered his children, 'educative, fertilising, in a degree which no other "intellectual experience" our youth was to know'. His acts of memory are many layered, and here he remembers anticipating the future, feeling a 'sharp and strange... quite heart-shaking little prevision'. He revives the small boy's 'splendour and terror of interest' to be associated with pictures by Guérin, Prudhon, David, and others, as a:

> foretaste... of all the fun, confusedly speaking, that one was going to have, and the kind of life... always of the queer so-called inward sort... that one was going to lead. It came of itself, this almost awful apprehension in all the presences, under our courier's protection and in my brother's company – it came just there and so; there was alarm in it somehow as well as bliss. The bliss in fact I think scarce disengaged itself at all, but only the sense of a freedom of contact and appreciation really too big for one, and leaving such a mark on the very place, the pictures, the frames themselves, the figures within them, the particular parts and features of each, the look of the rich light, the smell of the massively enclosed air, that I have never since renewed the old exposure without renewing again the old emotion and taking up the small scared consciousness. *That*, with so many of the conditions repeated, is the charm – to feel afresh the beginning of so much that was to be. (*SBO*, ch. 25)

James as memoirist is subtle, particular, sensuous, and analytic, pursuing his *recherche du temps perdu*, layering emotions of past and present, anticipation and memory, private and public life, with an intense joy. He delights in the acts of memory.

The memory offers special pleasures to the lover of his fiction. As it ramifies, small links with the novels appear, observed by reader, not writer. On rereading this first volume I noticed a version of that famous but obscure metaphor of the large loose baggy monster, an image so familiar that it is received with a groan instead of a scrutiny. The Parisian entertainment of the James children was subjected to some censorship and James relates how circuses were permitted while the French theatre, unlike the American and English, was not. He saw a show called

*Le Diable d'Argent* in which the *donnée* was

> the gradual shrinkage of the Shining One, a money-monster hugely inflated at first, to all the successive degrees of loose bagginess as he leads the reckless young man he has originally contracted with from dazzling pleasure to pleasure, till at last he is a mere shrivelled silver string such as you could almost draw through a keyhole. (*SBO*, ch. 26)

A Jamesian image cluster: money-monster, Paris, corruption, reckless young man, and loose bagginess. Or there is an account of Rachel's performance of *Phèdre* in which she appeared weighed down by heavy drapery, which James may have recalled when he describes Isabel Archer, first seen free and hatless in a garden, appearing after her marriage in her Florentine drawing-room, weighed down by a mass of drapery. Such images join the playful recall in *The American Scene* of the little red apples in New England orchards, like 'figures in the carpet', and its graver echo, in 'some beast that had sprung from the jungle' to describe the problem of race. (The context makes any racist undertone unlikely.) James's cornucopia of images spills from fiction into non-fiction and back again.

The central register of consciousness shows itself most complexly in what must have been the awkward scenes, for the recalling author, of the Civil War. In that war Wilky was wounded and Robertson (Bob) fought bravely, cousins and other contemporaries were killed. The younger brothers write home to their civilian elders, in relaxed slangy narratives, war correspondents memorialized by the brother whose 'obscure hurt' keeps him at home. (The incident remains one of the undisclosed secrets in James, like those in his novels.) The experience of the war was political as well as personal; James makes plain the abolitionist sympathies of family and friends. Wilky commanded a regiment of black soldiers, and writes his footnote to the history of American race relations. James narrates news of the war through a filter of memory which he knows is romantic, and through these unromantic family documents, joins memory of the past with its present-tense soldiers' reports.

As in the novels, there is a doubled narrative – the story, and the story of its telling and listening. James is not really departing from his structural principle of economy, and foreshortens in the interests of decent personal reserve. These recollections turned out to be what he had always wanted and never managed to write, the history of a story-seeker's imagination, laid aside until he came to struggle with the miscellany of this recall. He tells how the Civil War narratives, highly foreshortened, relate 'the drama of the War' where his was only a 'visionary assistance' – the French nuance coming in handy. The self-abnegating narrator expresses the civilian's longing, compassion, and inhibition, creating a reticent medium in which imaginative caring is a presence in absence, keeping some continuity in a miscellaneous narrative, and showing his awareness of the difficult enterprise:

> I am sure I thought more things under that head, with the fine visionary ache, than I thought in all other connections together; for the simple reason that one had to *ask* leave – of one's own spirit – for these last intermissions, whereas one but took it, with both hands free, for one's sense of the bigger cause. (*NSB* XI)

'One's sense of the bigger cause': this is an older man recalling a young man's war, a war in which he played a listener's part, far from the action, aware of his own youth and distance, tactful, awkward, yet seeing the art in the telling. Now he compounds spectatorship, recording young deaths, as he was to lament others in the First World War 'wanting, never ceasing to want, to "do" something for them, set as upright and clear-faced as may be, each in his sacred niche' (*NSB* VII).

The title – *Notes of a Son and Brother* – announces a modesty found for the war-narratives' wealth of quoted documentation, and for his chronicle of a father's and a brother's life. But the memoirs also tell his own story – external events, like the injury, choices in education, the change from law to authorship, dissatisfaction with America and choice of Europe, and inner events, like the recurring nightmare located in the *Galérie d'Apollon* of the Louvre, where James's dream-ego becomes the hunter, not the hunted, already mentioned as a link with 'The Jolly Corner' and a model for reciprocal structure. James has been criticized for cutting and altering the letters of Mary Temple, and he also played fast and loose with other letters, including William's, defending himself on aesthetic grounds when criticized by his nephew. His editorial appropriations are deplorable from our standpoint, but they were a habit of his time and his personal insistence on revision.

Though there is the emphasis on the story-seeker's progress and the history of that man of imagination, the narrative has tremendous range and elasticity. It is about others as well as the small boy, about father and mother, siblings, cousins, authors, actors, and unknown soldiers. Its rich and flowing particularization contrasts with the elaborately generalizing *American Scene* and the taut fictions. As an autobiographer James is flexible, witty, and inventive, varying his distance from materials, intelligently aware of past and present emotions without losing touch with them. He modulates from a matter-of-fact tone, neither modest nor immodest, treating self as subject and object, to a restrained pity and affection for other people, places, and times. This reflexive autobiography is original in construction, like his novels, looking ahead to experiments in biography like those of Sartre, and the pseudo-autobiographical novels of Proust. As a study of James's beginnings, in life and art, there can be no better book.

# 10

# The Literary Critic

James wrote literary criticism from the beginning. He began reviewing in his early twenties, concentrating on novels. He deplored the absence of 'any critical treatise upon fiction' in his first piece for the *North American Review* in 1864, after drifting away from his study of law at Harvard (*Life*, i. 175). The reviews were quickly joined by short stories and eventually, in the next decade, by the novels, but he remained a stylish and knowledgeable critic, sought after by editors. Literary journalism, like travel-writing, was an important source of his earnings. He was a reviewer of painting and drama, rarely of poetry, and most influentially of novels, doing for his art what Aristotle did for tragedy and Coleridge for Shakespeare and Wordsworth.

Like many English novelists from Defoe onwards, James began as a journalist, and his reviewing was intimately related to his creative writing in a way which continued throughout his life. He learnt to write as a journalist, needing to shape and enliven his prose in the business of attracting readers. Though his style grew less concise and more mannered, he remains one of the few entertaining literary critics. When he read his lecture on Browning, 'The Novel in *The Ring and the Book*', the audience murmured with pleasure at his language. He followed a standard of excellence set in America by such editors as Charles Eliot Norton, Edwin Lawrence Godkin, W. D. Howells, and James Russell Lowell, and in England by such critics as A. E. Dallas, G. H. Lewes and Marian Evans, who offered knowledge, intelligent judgement, and style. The Victorian novelists – Thackeray, Dickens, George Eliot – learnt their trade in brief pieces intended to amuse, often sheltering under an absence of signature. As Roger Gard says, introducing *Henry James. The Critical Muse: Selected Literary Criticism*, James's 'literary criticism is so vivacious, informative, and elegant that few readers will find it other than a pleasure to read'.

Gard contrasts two main responses to James's criticism: an exaggerated attention to the theoretical implications and influences of the Preface to the New York Edition, and Leavis's view of James as a pragmatic, impressionistic, and occasional critic, whose work, 'was determined by his own creative preoccupations'. (You could turn this round and say that his novels were determined by his grasp of structural principle but I don't think we can distinguish cause and effect in James's case.) Leavis was criticized by Vivien Jones in *James the Critic*, as appropriating James for an 'aggressively untheoretical criticism of moral evaluation by rejecting the Prefaces'. Rebuking Jones for simplifying Leavis and overrating the Prefaces, Gard regrets that Leavis's essay on James was used as preface for Morris Shapira's collection *Henry James: Selected Literary Criticism*, which reprinted 'disproportionately much of James's dismissals of various types of aestheticism'. He believes the debate represents extremes of response and judgement likely to be felt 'at different but quickly succeeding times, by any alert reader', concluding that James reconciled a life-based and an art-defending view of fiction, steering a 'middle way... not... of timid mediocrity but of reconciling critical genius'. Gard's is a valuable reminder that James the formalist is concerned with the art of rendering life. But questionings of mimesis in the second half of this century make it possible to see James's views on fiction, stated in critical essays and revealed in novels, in a way which avoids this polarity of formalism and realism.

Though not even appearing to be a mimetic novelist – as George Eliot, for instance, does – James is passionately concerned with what he carefully calls not realism but 'the air of reality' ('The Art of Fiction', *CM*, no. 26). He insists on it in the early reviews, 'The New Novel', the lectures on Balzac and Browning, and the Prefaces. His discovery of refraction through a centre of consciousness allows him to be realistic or mimetic while admitting into the novel a principle of conspicuous fiction-making, though he does not formulate it in these terms. But he was a theorist, always deploring critics' neglect of the art of fiction. His criticism was unusually theoretical for its time, concerned with form as well as mimesis, and one of his great attractions as a theorist is the detached and intimate use of his own writing for structural analysis. This gives his analysis a special tone, an unabstract, vivid, terminology. Gard stresses the inseparability of James's metaphorical wit from his thinking, in examples chiefly drawn from the occasional pieces, but it is also the great brightener and lightener of his discussions of form.

Seeing character as functional, for instance, is an abstract formulation, but James turns it into the animated figure of a carriage, with some figures seated as privileged passengers, others only wheels that run and roll. Looking, in 'The New Novel' (1914) (*CM*, no. 76), at Conrad's narrators and listeners, as they compound narrative speculation, he calls them the 'tell-tale little dogs', and I have already mentioned the startling comparison of refracted narrative to the shadow of a plane's wings in the same article. He thinks in pictures. His criticism is a creator's criticism, sensuous as well as intellectual, like Coleridge's. He is as amusing a critic as he is a novelist, using the same individual voice, not using the language of abstraction. Making up his language as he goes along, he articulates the trajectory of a response, in words conveying affection and pleasure, or dismay and hostility, moved but sufficiently detached to categorize. These qualities are present from the beginning, but it is in the discussions of form that they are most unusual and valuable.

James was a brilliant reviewer, judicial and personal, harsh and generous, but never too harsh or too generous. All his criticism is the work of someone who cares intensely about the novel. The voice and feeling are less rapturous and private than his astonishingly excited and intimate addresses to a Muse – *mon bon* – in the notebooks, but are stirred by passion. His early work is not just pragmatic: the 'Art of Fiction', written in response to Walter Besant's *Art of Fiction*, in 1884, is the beginning of a fervent effort to treat the novel with the seriousness directed to poetry and drama. But many of its famous utterances about the indissolubility of character, plot, and incident, and the relationship of art to life, are made excitingly specific in the detailed, patient, detached examinations of his own work in the Prefaces, and it is that discussion which is central to James's originality as the founder of modern criticism of fiction – perhaps of other genres too.

In the later writing there are important shifts in emphasis. For example, 'The Art of Fiction' asserts an organic unity in which character, incident, picture, narrative, and description are all inextricably joined. 'A novel', he says, 'is a living thing, all one and continuous, like any other organism, and in proportion as it lives will it be found, I think that in each of the parts will be found something of each of the other parts'. This is a valuable restatement of Coleridge's formulation of the relation of part to whole in Shakespeare or Wordsworth, and its application to fiction treats the Cinderella genre analytically and judiciously.

He later comes to look closely at the texts he knows most intimately, after a gap in time which makes him reader as well as writer, of context as well as text, past as well as present. In the Prefaces he makes distinctions not dreamt of in the reply to Besant, between elements of fiction which are means and others that are ends. Instead of saying that everything in a novel is illustrative, he says some things are more illustrative than others. In 'The Art of Fiction' he says, 'I cannot imagine composition existing in a series of blocks', but in the Prefaces that is precisely how he does see composition. The Preface to *The Wings of the Dove* (*CM*, no. 69) says:

> There was all the 'fun', to begin with, of establishing one's successive centres – of fixing them so exactly that the portions of the subject commanded by them as by happy points of view, and accordingly treated from them, would constitute, so to speak, sufficiently solid *blocks* of wrought material, squared to the sharp edge, as to have weight and mass and carrying power.... Such a block... is the whole preliminary presentation of Kate Croy.

This building imagery is frequent here and in the Prefaces to *The Portrait of a Lady* and *The Awkward Age*, with related images of architecture, theatre, and painting. He has not rejected organicism, but he has refined and redefined his concept of artistic unity, analysing components with a practitioner's sense of composition.

It is as a critic of his own fiction that his influence is established. The Prefaces he wrote for the New York Edition of his novels and stories, published between 1907 and 1909, have been reprinted in several selections, those by Shapira and Gard, the collection edited by R. P. Blackmur as *The Art of the Novel*, and reprints of the novels. The Prefaces, essays like 'The New Novel', revaluations of French novelists, a few reviews, and the notebooks, offer the most important analysis of narrative form in the first half of the twentieth century. James's preoccupations turn up in later theoretical and textual criticism, and when we look back at Victorian and Edwardian criticism of fiction, before and during James's time, it is plain that he is the novel's first analytic critic. His work was used and popularized by his editor and friend Percy Lubbock, whose *Craft of Fiction* (1921) was one of the few 'treatises on fiction' available in the pre-war and war years, Jamesian in analytic method and judgement, and elegantly retelling the great stories. When I read it as an undergraduate, it took me at once to James.

James contemplates his own work in a way which is probably unique, as he rereads and rewrites it. Always an imagistic critic, he recycles the imagery of his fiction in his Prefaces and later essays in a remarkable way. Rereading *The Portrait of a Lady,* he transfer the poetics of architecture from novel to Preface, then in later novels he revises it again: the house, the room, the corridor, and the window are spatial symbols invented by Isabel Archer and Maggie Verver, in collaboration with their narrator, and they become terms in James's narratives of composition, his analysis and judgement of form and genre, his criticism of Wells and Conrad, and his defence of the novel's elastic art. His rhetoric is functional, persuasive, and illuminating, as he thinks out his theory of form. A common imagery bonds criticism with fiction. His work is all of a piece. Those who want to see the novel as scientific, and criticism as narrative and imagistic, will find support in James's generic fluidities of discourse.

James began as a young reviewer sounding like an old judge, praising Scott and deprecating Dickens with an air of authority, scrupulously weighing words, speaking out of literary and historical knowledge. I don't suggest that the magisterial voice is spurious, far from it: the grand manner of this very young man is amusing, but he gets away with it because of fresh perception and example, far-ranging fact and sheer intelligence. He writes as someone who knows the books backwards. I often disagree with him, but he always says something sharp and deep. He judges his own work with stunning detachment, writing from a deep inwardness with its history, and a care for the craft.

Of course, like any artist, he is publicizing and promoting his own art and methods. He does this less conspicuously in the early reviews, but it is present, because he is reviewing as an ambitious artist, writing reviews and stories at the same time. Shrewdly criticizing Dickens's representation of society in *Our Mutual Friend* as a 'community of eccentrics', when the whole point of 'society' is conformity to rule (*CM*, no. 6), he speaks for the sociological imagination which was to create the seedy rich parties in *The Wings of the Dove*, *The Ambassadors*, and *The Sacred Fount*, where the society is as greedy, self-indulgent, hypocritical, and snobbish as the Veneerings, but disguised and distinguished by elegant conformity, superior to eccentricity. That is his point. Dickens gets an unfair review as James studies social representation. When in the shrewd witty lines of '"Daniel Deronda" A Conversation' Constantius objects that the novel shows 'views' on life instead of life, he speaks for a writer whose gift for abstraction never shows in dialogue, and not often in narrative (*CM*, no. 18). (The Wildean views and manner of Gabriel Nash in *The Tragic Muse* form an exception which proves a rule, as the novel does itself, in theme and form.) Interestingly, Edward L. Burlingame in the *North American Review* (Sept. 1877) and an anonymous writer in the *Eclectic Review* (Aug. 1877) say almost the same about James's *The American*.

What James says about Balzac, Zola, Tolstoy, Edith Wharton, Wells, Bennett, and Hugh Walpole is consistent with his values and practice. When he writes to Wharton and Walpole, trying to be nice to his friends, critical sternness gets the upper hand. If his critical response seems surprising, in his admiration of *Kipps*, Gissing, Stevenson, Zola, there is a reason in his fiction. The affinities or links are not always explicit, but they are there to be discovered. He does not lack empathy, but his overriding concern is with his ideal of artistic conscience. He is a thoroughly consistent critic and artist, always on duty.

Self-analysis develops in the Prefaces. From the accumulated particulars of the novels that he rereads, with pleasure, surprise, chagrin, and admiration, and rewrites, emerge generalizations, then definitions of form and genre. His insistence on visible shape and unity, economy of form and total relevance, is also a reaction against contemporary fiction. In his self-critique and his criticism of other novelists he voices grievances against the Victorians, though he loves and admires the writers who delighted his youth, and nourished his art too. He is saturated in Dickens, Thackeray, and George Eliot. Even Trollope, whom he dislikes, he knows thoroughly. Never was there such a devoted anti-Victorian.

His Isabel Archer owes much to Gwendolen Harleth, as Leavis showed, though also much to Maggie Tulliver and Dorothea Brooke. Some of his best comic, grotesque, and pathetic characters, Henrietta Stackpole, Millicent Hemming, Madame Grandoni, would not exist without Dickens – though other comic characters are more Thackerayan, comic without being grotesque, like Bob Assingham, the Pococks, and the nameless narrator of *The Sacred Fount*. In *The Wings of the Dove*, crammed with the conspicuous consumption Thackeray loved to catalogue, price, and judge, James unsurprisingly links Kate Croy with the Thackerayan heroine, thinking of Ethel Newcome, and also Becky Sharp and Blanche Amory, for whom, he lamented, Thackeray lacked the love Balzac felt for *sa Valérie*. The great Victorians mark a valuable negative for James, act as stop-signals of life without art, wasteful manner, loose form, terrible fluidity, a leak in the interest. He makes such rejections explicitly, but implicitly too, in his concision, economy, total relevance, symmetry, and asserted rhetoric.

He gave modernism a language as it was beginning to develop. For half a century, with the brilliant help of Lubbock, who wrote about him and for him, he turned critics and students away from the Victorian novel, persuading them by example and argument that such 'large loose baggy monsters' (*CM*, no. 60) as Thackeray, Dumas, Tolstoy, George Eliot, and Dickens, whom he admired with reservations, were story-tellers not artists, leading them to judge the multiple plot as rambling and disordered, the omniscient narrator as 'intrusive', dismissible as an element of matter not manner. Until the late 1950s this was the assumption in George Eliot criticism, and still occasionally crops up. Other novelist-critics, D. H. Lawrence and Virginia Woolf, for instance, have written a subjective and self-promoting critique of their genre but they have not strongly influenced critical opinion. Only James Joyce's influence on ideas of impersonality and multi-vocalism has made a critical impact as radical as James's. He helped to make critics look at the novel's form, but his single-minded promotion of that form as he saw and made it was bad news for the study of his Victorian ancestors, though if it proceeds from an anxiety about influence, it is well disguised as superiority.

James introduced new structural concepts into the criticism of fiction. They have formed the basis of much of our theory and analytic practice: point of view, voice, functional character, foreshortening, anticipation, and unity are all concepts explicitly developed in the critical analysis and theory of prose narrative which James formed or helped to form. They were developed in the solvent of performance. When he formulates points of view, as 'centre' and 'consciousness', it is with Roderick Mallett's, through whom Roderick Hudson and other characters are imagined, as example (*CM*, no. 56). When he discusses characters belonging to form rather than subject, the subject comes up as he judges Henrietta Stackpole and Maria Gostrey to have been overtreated (*CM*, no. 70). When he speaks of major and minor characters (as in *CM*, no. 56), there is the sense of character as construct, aesthetically adjusted as part of the whole unified work of art: it is not enough for Mary Garland to be a realistic character, but necessary for her and her habitat to balance the presence and background of Christina Light. James joins the theatrical and poetic reactions against Bradleyan character-criticism to make us see character as rhetoric not reality. Whatever he says about the air of reality, he makes it clear that mimesis is an inadequate concept.

When *Middlemarch* is judged 'a treasure-house of details, but . . . an indifferent whole' (*CM*, no. 11), I hope we disagree, but we know what he means. He is comparing it with the streamlined and symmetrical elegance of his novels. Their symmetries and antithesis are as plain as in a lyric, their scenes contrast like those in a well-made play, their narrators are subdued and disguised, to promote scene and dialogue, their scheme of total relevance charges every object and act so that characters cannot put on the light or eat fruit without symbolic meaning. Criticism has taken its time to shed his insistence on norms of concentration and unity. Wayne Booth's *The Rhetoric of Fiction*, W. J. Harvey's *The Art of George Eliot*, and my *Novels of George Eliot* and *The Appropriate Form* all argued a case against this insistence, analysing a variety of voice and form, defending the loose, fluid, and episodic three-volume novel against James's charge of redundancy, waste, and looseness, proposing a more flexible concept of novelistic structure. Since those critiques of the late 1950s and early 1960s, structuralist theories have classified and standardized the concepts of form, and post-structuralism eroded ideas of closure, unity, and organicism. James needed to pursue his own ideal of 'a deep-breathing economy and an organic form' (Preface to *The Tragic Muse*, *CM*, no. 60), and the old New Critical ideas and methods created a climate in which he won admiration for his novels and his criticism, as Blackmur's edition of the Prefaces makes especially clear. Once we have placed that criticism and shown its limits, it can be appreciated for what it is, an idea of form which applies to some artists not to all, but an idea which can be expanded and modified.

James is the promoter of conspicuous form, a displayed mannerism and flourish which Auden calls Gongorist (in his 1946 introduction to *The American Scene*), a visible unity and symmetry which his symbolic titles announce and his dynamic symbols help to create. James's concentration had many origins. There were the living examples of Flaubert and Turgenev, whom he knew, and whose pursuit of the art of fiction was an inspiration and a counter-model for a reader brought up on Dickens and Scott. There was the devotion to painting and architecture which we can see in his travel writings and reviews of exhibitions, developing his taste for conspicuous unity. Most ironic, in view of his failure in the genre, is his passion for theatre, rooted in his experience of the stage as a young child, first in New York, then in Paris. James cultivated the right word, like Flaubert, and the right construction. He chose to concentrate, in the genre in which such concentration is optional, as the painter and dramatist are forced to concentrate by the compulsions of their genre.

He gave – or helped to give – modern criticism its method and techniques. The New Criticism's interpretation of dominant themes and analysis of symmetry, balance, antithesis, imagery, and symbolism are all present in the New York Prefaces, as James sets new readings against old ones, in an unprecedentedly sustained retrospect. Of course James was not the first novelist to make images dominate and draw attention to prevailing themes. Dickens and George Eliot did so before him, and, though influenced by Ibsen, as Michael Egan shows, James had earlier models before him too. His last novels remind us of Ibsen's symbolic phenomena, but the sprawling Victorians were also symbolists, though Ibsen's economy and fantasy made him especially attractive to James, despite an uncongenial didacticism.

James's critical ideas get into his stories as well as his Prefaces.

'The Figure in the Carpet' is a tease and a temptation for critics, who cannot resist trying to guess what they cannot possibly guess, the undisclosed key figure of an invented and imaginary *œuvre*. The idea of such a key figure, its image taken from the spatial art of oriental carpet-making, may have helped to develop that interest in image-patterns which started with Shakespeare criticism. Joseph Frank's idea of spatial form clearly derived from James's practice, perhaps from this famous story whose novelist and whose critic take so readily to the idea of a key figure. James anticipates the critic's enthusiasm for staking a claim to hermeneutic discovery, in playful but baleful putting-down of critical hubris. James knew that a search for a key to a work, or all the works, turns students of fiction into critical Casaubons.

The story turns on that fashionable item, the absence. James is probably the first novelist to encourage the idea of absences, though Meredith is a rival. James puts absences in conspicuous places – the figure in the carpet, Amerigo and Charlotte in Italy, the scandalous behaviour of Lionel Croy, the object manufactured in Woollett, the name of Milly's illness – aren't these the first significant gaps in American and European fiction? As we ponder those essays claiming to discover the carpet's figure and Woollett's object – R. W. Stallman knows it is a watch – we should recall James's case in 'The Figure in the Carpet' against the avidity of critics. There are many motives for making holes in the fabric of art, and the contrivance of elegant revenge is not James's only one. James is, of course, interested in avoiding omniscience, so cuts down information severely, anticipating the *scriptible* novel of Roland Barthes. He also sees the funny side of refusing to tell, and the joke, like his other jokes, is good because it is ingenious, serious and ambiguous, sometimes refusing to disclose that it is a joke. Jamesian uncertainty is nothing to do with Heisenberg, whose name is sometimes taken in vain by critics avid for structural subversions, but it is subversive.

One way or another, he was ripening modern theory. While he explicitly insists on unity and organic form, what he does as a novelist is to make spaces, ask questions, present enigmas, and leave endings open. He encourages the reader to construct as well as receive, in Barthean terms, to write as well as read. Most graceful of formalists, he can delight in breaking a line, forcing a discord, opening an ending, ruffling a smoothness. We are beginning to catch up with him, and since the author of his super-subtle ghost-stories must be a ghost on whom nothing is lost, a recognition of that irony may compensate for the obtuseness of his contemporaries.

Those critics grumbled at his obscurity, and it was with James – unless it was with Browning or Meredith – that the obscurity of modern literature arrived. Obscurity is relative: perhaps a better word is difficulty. The difficulty of James is the product of his closely observed and pondered enquiry into imagination, in and outside art.

It is a function of a complex analysis of method, medium, form, and mind, which anticipates the central reflexiveness of modern art, articulated by Barthes and other theorists. Reflexiveness is present in Victorian fiction too, and is, I think, only quantitatively a sign of twentieth-century art, in modernist or, more conspicuously, post-modernist self-consciousness. James's reflexive art is complex and various. As I have said, his novels and stories are never thinly concerned with the special subject of art and the artist. Though the subject of art is prominent, and the concern with imagination central, James insisted that the novelist should write as a historian, not an inventor. He disliked extremes of authorial self-consciousness, criticizing Trollope (in *Century Magazine*, in July 1883 (*CM*, no. 23)) for insisting on his fiction-making within the fiction: 'He took a suicidal satisfaction in reminding the reader that the story he was telling, was only, after all, a make-believe.' In the next year, he repeated the criticism in 'The Art of Fiction': 'He admits that the events he narrates have not really happened, and that he can give his narrative any turn the reader may like best. Such a betrayal of a sacred office seems to me, I confess, a terrible crime . . .'.

James wrote a number of stories dealing with the novelist's art, mostly in his earlier period. 'The Lesson of the Master', 'The Death of the Lion', and 'The Figure in the Carpet' are subtly amusing self-analysing stories about acts and arts of writing, reading, and interpreting. The figure of the artist, however, is always dramatized indirectly, with a double advantage, from James's point of view. The subject of narration is put at a distance from the reader, making no claims to verisimilitude or flexible artifice; and the making of the fiction is the subject of the story. The narrator sometimes speaks in a first person, but is kept on a tight rein by scope and selection, never constituting what James in the Preface to *The Tragic Muse* called 'a leak in the interest'. Such narrators are never omniscient, but struggle to carry out difficult or impossible enquiries into the nature of art and the artist. They allow James to assume the most interesting of his absences, the absence of the author-surrogate, the dominant teller.

James loved to fuse event and character, and these stories are frequently about making out a story. In 'The New Novel' James praised Conrad for the refracted narrative in *Chance*, which created the 'fusion between what we are to know and that prodigy of our knowing which is ever half the beauty of the atmosphere of authenticity'. Not for James Conrad's 'reciter', that 'definite responsible intervening first-person singular, possessed of infinite sources of reference, who immediately proceeds to set up another, to the end that this other may conform again to the practice', but his admiration for the 'reciting' construction of *Chance* springs from his own affection for structures of enquiry and speculation. In the short fiction the reciters are sometimes definite and developed, sometimes even a literary voice, but in the novels his structures are very different from Conrad's, though they, too, are designed to fuse subject and object of knowing. In James as in Conrad the characters try to find each other's secrets and understand each other's mysteries. These are true epistemological narratives. The story in them, usually of more magnitude than in 'The Story in It', may be a story of ordinary life. In the quiet delicacy of 'The Story in It', James is like Wordsworth in 'Goody Blake', trying to make his reader see 'a tale in everything'. His minimal narrative may be a paradigm for art, but also brings out the telling and listening in every life.

He wrote with fine enthusiasm about 'Ivan Turgenev' (*CM*, no. 40), whom he called 'the novelists' novelist': 'His vision is of the world of character and feeling, the world of relations life throws up at every hour and on every spot . . . his air is that of the great central region of passion and motive, of the usual, the inevitable, the intimate – the intimate for weal or woe.'

James's social range is much more restricted than Turgenev's, but he wrote warmly about his friend's influential social sympathies, and if the creator of Miss Pynsent, Hyacinth's foster-mother, the clerk 'In the Cage', and the cheeky couple in 'The Papers' draws fewer humble characters like Turgenev's, his occasional humble people and some of the grander ones are images of 'the usual, the inevitable, the intimate'. Lacking the astonishing naturalness of Turgenev's attachment 'to the misery, the simplicity, the piety, the patience, of the unemancipated peasant', James loved Turgenev – who never responded to his admirer's work – in a response to political feeling as well as artistry.

James's late criticism refined and qualified his utterances about organic form. His development of influential critical concepts took his lifetime, and crowned his achievement. But for him, life and form go hand in hand, and this is seen in the development of his historical sense. 'The Jolly Corner', the three great novels, and the unfinished fiction show a clear sense of the making of character by circumstance, and there is a parallel insight in his literary criticism. It is not prominent in the Prefaces, where the emphasis is placed on form and technique, but it is present in several essays on other novelists. Like Thackeray, James was a member of the Reform Club, and, like Thackeray's, his attitude to reform cannot be judged by his hob-nobbing with *le beau monde*. Sidney Waterlow, one of his Rye friends, reports him wondering 'how so complete and cumbrous a thing as the British Empire managed to go on at all... perhaps it was simply easier for it to go on than to stop.... He felt tempted to call himself a rapid Socialist' (*Life*, 96). As a radical declaration, this echoes Thackeray's prediction that the scaffolding of society must be torn down, and Gerard Hopkins's famous 'red letter' to Robert Bridges.

James wrote an admiring review of Edith Wharton's *The Reef* (1912) (*CM*, no. 74), but criticizes it for locating an American story in a French habitat, 'the whole thing, unrelated and unreferred save in the most superficial way to its milieu and background, and to any determining or qualifying *entourage*'. He concludes that the social isolation works for her 'Racinian' characterization, but the comment on milieu is significant. The historic sense is central in a review of Emile Faguet's *Balzac* which appeared in the *Times Literary Supplement* in 1913, (*CM*, no. 75), in which he judges Balzac – for James, always the great novelist – to have been happy to have been born in his time, a time of historical visibilities, the 'later part of the eighteenth century, with the Revolution, the Empire, and the Restoration' showing with distinctness 'their separate marks and stigmas, their separate trails of character and physiognomic hits', less clearly differentiated to later generations confronted by 'fatal fusions and uniformities . . . the running together of . . . differences of form and tone . . . the ruinous liquefying wash of the great industrial brush'. Balzac's strength is in the grasp of creature in circumstance:

> What makes Balzac so pre-eminent and exemplary that he was to leave the novel a far other and a vastly more capacious and significant affair than he found it, is his having felt his fellow-creatures (almost altogether for him his contemporaries) as quite failing of reality, as swimming in the vague and the void and the abstract, unless their social conditions, to the last particular, their generative and contributive circumstances, of every discernible sort, enter for all these are 'worth' into his representative attempt. This great compound of the total looked into and starting up in its element, as it always does, to meet the eye of genius and patience half way, bristled for him with all its branching connections.

This passage is over-elaborate in style, teasing out shades of meaning, scrupulously but fussily, and muffling the main point: 'unless their social conditions . . . enter . . . into his representative attempt'. The word *representation* is an exact term in James, meaning solid specification. In the earlier 'Lesson of Balzac', published in the *Atlantic Monthly* in 1905 (*CM*, no. 56), he contrasts Balzacian realism with Zola's researched historicism, which he calls 'representation imitated', and in his 1903 tribute, 'Emile Zola' (*CM*, no. 50), 'the most extraordinary *imitation* of observation'.

James loved Balzac even more than he loved Turgenev, master of grace and economy, and his meditations on Balzac continue and mutate. His writings on Turgenev are not just about form, and the essay of 1896 (*CM* no. 40) shows his insistence on the novelist's social circumstance: he translates it into American terms, comparing the Russian nobleman to a 'Virginian or Carolinian slaveholder during the first half of the century', inclining to 'Northern views'. Compared with the comments on Balzac, Zola, and Wharton, the essay underplays history, admiring concision, 'the unity . . . of material and form', and the tender and ironic creation of an 'innermost' world. But history comes in, with the praised vision of the 'individual figure . . . in the general flood of life, steeped in all its relations and contacts, struggling or submerged, a hurried particle in the stream'. The historical sense was not new in James's criticism, any more than in his fiction, but in both it is more apparent in the later years, and directly, rather than indirectly, articulated.

Although Balzac is the master, 'pre-eminent and exemplary', James's deep affinity was with Turgenev, the visible model in the early work. The Preface to *A Portrait of a Lady* (*CM*, no. 58) shows how James meditated on Turgenev's tale of a novel's genesis and growth, from soliciting figure to peopled context. But one of his finest creations, Lewis Lambert Strether, was named after Balzac's *Louis Lambert*, and is the centre of one of James's most socially questioning novels. James is engaged in a perpetual dialogue with Turgenev the formalist and Balzac the historian, offering grateful homage to his two markedly different teachers.

It is a reticent homage, stated in his critical essays but understated in the late fiction. James's literary references are always thoroughly assimilated, part of the form and fabric of his art; they seem to have slowly reduced from the early ironic imitations of Tennysonian themes in 'A Landscape Painter' and 'A Day of Days', and the naming of George Eliot as an influence on Isabel Archer, to subdued echoes like the references to Thackeray and Maeterlinck in *The Wings of the Dove*, Blake's poem in *The Golden Bowl*, and the quiet naming in *The Ambassadors*. Strether was not to be a novelist, as James once intended, but he was to be tenderly and ironically named, in an Americanized version, after Balzac's eponymous hero, in one of many small links between James's criticism and his fiction. Like Turgenev, and unlike the artists – serious or just fashionable – whose self-reference is abstract, clever, imitative, and amoral, James is self-analytic and also amusing, individual, and moral. This is true of his criticism as well as his fiction, though as a critic he is capable of being absorbed in a response to other people's art. While we regret his failures to admire Jane Austen, much of Conrad, and *Sons and Lovers*, we must appreciate the sensibility which placed Balzac so high, knew Flaubert thoroughly, warmed to Stevenson and Zola, 'clung' to Gissing, and loved Turgenev.

There are many artists who are perceptive critics of their own work and other people's, less than a handful whose criticism matches their art. In criticism and fiction, James transforms the language and structures in which art contemplates society, history, and the personal life.

# Select Bibliography

## WORKS BY HENRY JAMES

### Collected Editions

*The Novels and Tales of Henry James* (New York: Charles Scribner's, 1907–9). Known as the 'New York Edition', this collection incorporates substantially revised texts and a series of specially written prefaces. Published in 24 volumes; 2 further volumes – *The Ivory Tower* and *The Sense of the Past* – were added in 1918.

*The Complete Plays of Henry James*, ed. Leon Edel (London: Rupert Hart-Davis, 1949).

*The Complete Tales of Henry James*, ed. Leon Edel, 12 vols. (London: Rupert Hart-Davis, 1962–4). This edition reproduces the text of the first book (or, where none appears, the first periodical) publication of James's tales, rather than the revised text of the New York Edition. Volumes xi and xii cover the period 1900–10.

*Henry James Letters*, ed. Leon Edel, 4 vols. (Cambridge, Mass.: Belknap Press, 1974–84). The widest collection of James's letters available.

*Literary Criticism*, ed. Leon Edel with the assistance of Mark Wilson, 2 vols. (New York: Library of America, 1984). The most comprehensive edition of James's critical writings. The first volume covers essays on English and American writers; the second covers European writers, and includes the Prefaces to the New York Edition.

*The Complete Notebooks of Henry James*, ed. with introductions and notes by Leon Edel and Lyall H. Powers (New York and Oxford: Oxford University Press, 1987). A scholarly edition of the notebooks, which includes James's lengthy initial 'Project' for *The Ambassadors*.

### Separate Editions

*The American* (1877), with an introduction, biographical sketch, and a selection of background materials and commentaries by Richard Poirier (New York: Bantam Books, 1971). Includes some early reviews of James.

*The Portrait of a Lady* (1881), ed. Robert D. Bamberg (New York and London: Norton, 1975).

*The Tragic Muse* (1890) (Harmondsworth: Penguin, 1988).

*The Soft Side* (London: Methuen, 1900). A collection of short stories.

*The Sacred Fount* (1901), ed. with an introduction by John Lyon (Harmondsworth: Penguin, 1994). An annotated paperback edition.

*The Wings of The Dove* (1902), ed. Donald J. Crowley and Richard A. Hocks (New York and London: Norton, 1978). A good scholarly edition which includes a useful selection of critical and contextual material.

*The Ambassadors* (1903), ed. S. P. Rosenbaum (2nd end., New York and London: Norton, 1994). A good scholarly edition.

*The Better Sort* (London: Methuen, 1903). A collection of short stories.

*William Wetmore Story and his Friends from Letters, Diaries, and Recollections* (1903) (London: Thames & Hudson, 1957).

*The Golden Bowl* (1904), with an introduction by Gore Vidal (Harmondsworth: Penguin, 1985). Reproduces the text of the New York Edition with annotations and James's Preface.

*English Hours* (London: Heinemann, 1905). A collection of James's earlier English travel writings.

*The Question of Our Speech, The Lesson of Balzac: Two Lectures* (Boston and New York: Houghton, Mifflin, 1905). Lectures delivered during James's American tour of 1904–5.

*The American Scene* (1907), ed. with an introduction by W. H. Auden (New York: Charles Scribner's, 1946). Also includes three of James's earlier American travel sketches.

*Italian Hours* (London: Heinemann, 1909). A collection of James's Italian travel sketches, mostly from the 1870s, but with some twentieth-century additions.

*The Finer Grain* (London: Methuen, 1910). A collection of short stories.

*The Outcry* (London: Methuen, 1911).

*A Small Boy and Others* (London: Macmillan, 1913).

*Notes of a Son and Brother* (London: Macmillan, 1914).

*Notes on Novelists* (London: J. M. Dent, 1914). A collection of James's later critical essays.

*The Ivory Tower* (London: Collins, 1917).

*The Middle Years* (London: Collins, 1917).

*The Sense of the Past* (London: Collins, 1917).

*Within the Rim, and Other Essays 1914–1915* (London: Collins, 1918). A collection of essays recording James's wartime experiences.

*The Art of the Novel: Critical Prefaces*, with an introduction by R. P. Blackmur (New York and London: Charles Scribner's, 1934). Brings together all of James's prefaces to the New York Edition.

*The Art of Travel: Scenes and Journeys in America, England, France and Italy from the Travel Writings of Henry James*, ed. with an introduction by Morton Dauwen Zabel (New York: Doubleday, 1958). A useful selection of James's travel writings, which includes chapters from *The American Scene*.

*Henry James: Selected Literary Criticism*, ed. Morris Shapira (London: Heinemann, 1963). Includes a preface by F. R. Leavis on 'James as Critic'.

*Henry James. The Critical Muse: Selected Literary Criticism*, ed. with an introduction by Roger Gard (Harmondsworth: Penguin, 1987). A widely available and wide-ranging selection of James's critical essays and prefaces from all periods of his career.

*The Jolly Corner and Other Tales*, ed. with an introduction by Roger Gard (Harmondsworth: Penguin, 1990). A useful paperback edition of some of James's late stories.

NOTE: Many of James's novels are available in a variety of paperback editions, besides those cited above.

## BIBLIOGRAPHY

Edel, Leon, and Laurence, Dan H., revised with the assistance of James Rambeau, *A Bibliography of Henry James* (3rd edn., Oxford: Clarendon Press, 1982). The standard bibliography of James's writings, including details of book and periodical publication.

Funston, Judith E., *Henry James, 1975–1987: A Reference Guide* (Boston: G. K. Hall, 1991). A bibliography of critical work published on James during this period.

McColgan, Kristin Pruitt, *Henry James, 1917–1959: A Reference Guide* (Boston: G. K. Hall, 1979). As previous entry.

Scura, Dorothy McInnis, *Henry James, 1960–1974: A Reference Guide* (Boston: G. K. Hall, 1979). As previous entries.

Taylor, Linda J., *Henry James, 1866–1916: A Reference Guide* (Boston: G. K. Hall, 1982). An invaluable source of information on contemporary responses to James. Lists articles and reviews published in American newspapers and periodicals during his lifetime.

## BIOGRAPHY

Edel, Leon, *Henry James* (London: Rupert Hart-Davis, 1953–72). Originally published in 5 volumes under the following subtitles: *The Untried Years, 1843–1870* (1953), *The Conquest of London, 1870–1883* (1962), *The Middle Years, 1884–1894* (1963), *The Treacherous Years, 1895–1901* (1969), and *The Master, 1901–1916* (1972). Still a monumental achievement, although many of Edel's biographical interpretations have become subject to recent criticism.

——— *The Life of Henry James*, 2 vols. (Harmondsworth: Penguin, 1977). A condensed and revised edition of Edel's biography.

Kaplan, Fred, *Henry James: The Imagination of Genius* (London: Hodder & Stoughton, 1992). The most recent biography of James's life, substantially revising Edel's account.

Matthiesson, F. O., *The James Family* (New York: Alfred A. Knopf, 1947). Sets Henry James in the context of his extraordinary family, and includes selections from the writings of his father, Henry James, Sr., his brother William, and his sister, Alice.

Seymour, Miranda, *A Ring of Conspirators: Henry James and his Literary Circle, 1895–1916* (London: Hodder & Stoughton, 1988). Offers an account of James's relations with other prominent literary figures during his later life.

## CRITICISM

NOTE: There is a vast amount of criticism devoted to James. The following selection, therefore, concentrates mainly upon recent studies of the later writings, but with the addition of a number of significant earlier texts.

Allen, Elizabeth, *A Woman's Place in the Novels of Henry James* (London: Macmillan, 1984). A study of the representation of women in James's fiction.

Anesko, Michael, *'Friction with the Market': Henry James and the Profession of Authorship* (New York and Oxford: Oxford University Press, 1986). Situates James's career in relation to the changing literary market of the late nineteenth and early twentieth centuries. One of the first critics to attempt to historicize James as a writer.

Bell, Ian F. A. (ed.), *Henry James: Fiction as History* (London: Vision Press, 1984). A valuable collection of essays written from a number of modern critical perspectives, but concentrating, for the most part, on the historical and cultural resonances of James's writings.

Besant, Walter, *The Art of Fiction* (London: Chatto and Windus, 1884).

Blackall, Jean Frantz, *Jamesian Ambiguity and The Sacred Fount* (Ithaca: Cornell University Press, 1965).

Booth, Wayne C., *The Rhetoric of Fiction* (Chicago and London: University of Chicago Press, 1961). A general study of fictional narrative, which refers extensively to James's use of 'unreliable narrators'.

Bosanquet, Theodora, *Henry James at Work* (London: Hogarth Press, 1924). A personal account of Bosanquet's experiences as James's amanuensis during his later years; sheds interesting light upon his methods of composition.

Bradbury, Nicola, *Henry James: The Later Novels* (Oxford: Clarendon Press, 1979). A close reading of James's twentieth-century fiction, which includes a chapter on the unfinished novels.

Cameron, Sharon, *Thinking in Henry James* (Chicago and London: University of Chicago Press, 1989). A theoretically informed study which revises previous interpretations of James's treatment of consciousness in the later novels.

Chatman, Seymour, *The Later Style of Henry James* (Oxford: Basil Blackwell, 1972). A detailed linguistic study of the peculiarities of James's later prose style.

Dupee, F. W. (ed.), *The Question of Henry James: A Collection of Critical Essays* (London: Allan Wingate, 1947). Offers a wide selection of the most influential critical views from the first half of the century. Includes essays by T. S. Eliot, Joseph Conrad, Percy Lubbock, and Edmund Wilson.

Eakin, Paul John, 'Henry James and the Autobiographical Act', in *Fictions in Autobiography: Studies in the Art of Self-Invention* (Princeton: Princeton University Press, 1985), ch. 2., pp. 56–125. An extensive reading of James's strategies of self-representation in the autobiographies.

Egan, Michael, *Henry James: The Ibsen Years* (London: Vision, 1972). Examines the influence of the Norwegian playwright Henrik Ibsen on the development of James's writings.

Frank, Joseph, 'Spatial Form in Modern Literature', *Sewanee Review*, 53/2–4 (1945).

Freedman, Jonathan, *Professions of Taste: Henry James, British Aestheticism, and Commodity Culture* (Stanford: Stanford University Press, 1990). An important recent study which demonstrates James's continuing engagement with the concerns and figures of late-nineteenth-century aestheticism.

Gard, Roger, (ed.), *Henry James: The Critical Heritage* (London: Routledge & Kegan Paul, 1968). A valuable collection of critical responses to James, ranging from early reviews of the novels to later essays.

Geismar, Maxwell, *Henry James and his Cult* (London: Chatto & Windus, 1964). An iconoclastic study of James and his literary reputation.

Goode, John (ed.), *The Air of Reality: New Essays on Henry James* (London: Methuen, 1972). A useful collection of essays with James's later novels well represented.

Graham, Kenneth, *Henry James, The Drama of Fulfilment: An Approach to the Novels* (Oxford: Clarendon Press, 1975). Contains an extensive reading of *The Wings of the Dove*.

Grewal, O. P., *Henry James and the Ideology of Culture: A Critical Study of The Bostonians, The Princess Casamassima, and The Tragic Muse* (Academic Foundation Delhi, 1990).

Habegger, Alfred, *Henry James and the 'Woman Business'* (Cambridge: Cambridge University Press, 1989). Concentrates mainly on James's earlier life and fiction, but offers a provocative account of James's attitude towards women writers, and his understanding of sexual difference in general.

Hardy, Barbara, *The Novels of George Eliot: A Study in Form* (New York:

Oxford University Press, repr. 1963).

——— *The Appropriate Form: An Essay on the Novel* (London: Athlone Press, 1964). See the first two chapters for a discussion of James's use and conception of literary form.

——— *Tellers and Listeners: The Narrative Imagination* (London: Athlone Press, 1975).

——— 'Henry James: Reflexive Passions', in *Forms of Feeling in Victorian Fiction* (London: Peter Owen, 1985), 191–215.

——— *The Collected Essays of Barbara Hardy, i. Narrators and Novelists* (Brighton: Harvester, 1987). See 'The Nature of Narrative' and 'Objects in Novels', pp. 1–30.

——— 'Henry James: Imagining Imagination', in *Proceedings of the British Academy*, lxxiv (1988), 71–87.

Harvey, W. J., *The Art of George Eliot* (London: Chatto and Windus, 1961).

Holland, Lawrence, *The Expense of Vision: Essays on the Craft of Henry James* (Princeton: Princeton University Press, 1964).

Horne, Philip, *Henry James and Revision: The New York Edition* (Oxford: Clarendon Press, 1990). A detailed study of James's processes of textual revision.

Iser, Wolfgang, *The Act of Reading: A Theory of Aesthetic Response* (Baltimore and London: Johns Hopkins University Press, 1978). An important work of literary theory which uses James's story 'The Figure in The Carpet' (1896) as a model text in elaborating the practice of 'reader-response' criticism.

Jameson, Fredric, *The Political Unconscious: Narrative as a Socially Symbolic Act* (London: Methuen, 1981). Although referring only briefly (and contentiously) to James, this is a seminal work of modern critical theory, which combines formal and historical analysis of key literary texts.

Jones, Vivien, *James the Critic* (London and Basingstoke: Macmillan, 1984). One of the few book-length studies of James's literary criticism. Includes a chapter on the Prefaces to the New York Edition.

Krook, Dorothea, *The Ordeal of Consciousness in Henry James* (Cambridge: Cambridge University Press, 1962). In its time one of the most notable studies of consciousness in James's fiction.

Leavis, F. R., *The Great Tradition: George Eliot, Henry James, Joseph Conrad* (London: Chatto & Windus, 1948). Contains a well-known depreciation of James's later writings.

Lubbock, Percy, *The Craft of Fiction* (London: Jonathan Cape, 1921; repr. 1965). A study of fictional technique which was extremely influential in the development of James criticism.

Lustig, T. J., *Henry James and the Ghostly* (Cambridge: Cambridge University Press, 1994). A recent study of the 'supernatural' in James's fiction.

Matthiessen, F. O., *Henry James: The Major Phase* (London: Oxford

University Press, 1946). This influential study initiated the view that James's three major twentieth-century novels represent his crowning achievement.

Posnock, Ross, *The Trial of Curiosity: Henry James, William James, and the Challenge of Modernity* (New York and Oxford: Oxford University Press, 1991). An important, revisionary study of the twentieth-century writings, which examines the relationship between James's social and aesthetic thought and the philosophy of his brother William.

Rimmon, Schlomith, *The Concept of Ambiguity: The Example of James* (Chicago and London: Chicago University Press, 1977). A structuralist reading of ambiguity in James's fiction, with an extensive analysis of *The Sacred Fount*.

Rowe, John Carlos, *The Theoretical Dimensions of Henry James* (Wisconsin: University of Wisconsin Press, 1984). Applies modern literary theory to a selection of James's texts, mainly from the nineteenth century. A useful book which illustrates a variety of different strategies for reading James.

Sears, Sallie, *The Negative Imagination: Form and Perspective in the Novels of Henry James* (Ithaca: Cornell University Press, 1968). A study of the three major twentieth-century novels.

Sedgwick, Eve Kosofsky, 'The Beast in The Closet: James and the Writing of Homosexual Panic', in *Epistemology of the Closet* (Hemel Hempstead: Harvester Wheatsheaf, 1991), 182–212. Examines the cultural construction of homosexual anxiety and desire in James's story 'The Beast in the Jungle'. This essay has been widely discussed in recent James criticism.

Seltzer, Mark, *Henry James and the Art of Power* (Ithaca and London: Cornell University Press, 1984). Informed by the work of the historian Michel Foucault, this is a challenging study of the political and ideological imperatives contained within James's literary texts.

Stallman, R. W., *The Houses that James Built and Other Literary Studies* (Michigan: Michigan University Press, 1961). Includes a discussion of the theme of time in *The Ambassadors*.

Tanner, Tony (ed.), *Henry James: Modern Judgements* (London: Macmillan, 1968). A collection of critical essays on James.

——— *Henry James III: 1899–1916* (Writers and their Work, original series; Windsor: Profile Books, 1981).

Williams, Merle A., *Henry James and the Philosophical Novel: Being and Seeing* (Cambridge: Cambridge University Press, 1993). A recent study which explores the relationship between James's later novels and contemporary movements in philosophy.

Yeazell, Ruth Bernard, *Language and Knowledge in the Late Novels of Henry James* (Chicago and London: University of Chicago Press, 1976).

# Index